IGNITE YOUR SOUL, RELEASE YOUR MIND

Vol. 1

Ignite Your Soul, Release Your Mind Vol. 1
© 2013 by Mario Gabriel Adame

All Rights Reserved.
No part of this book may be reproduced in any written, electronic, recording, or photocopying form without written permission of the poet.

Dead Poets Dream Publishing, San Antonio, TX

ISBN: 0615929443
ISBN-13: 978-0615929446

Ignite Your Soul, Release Your Mind

Vol. 1

Mario Gabriel Adame

DEDICATION

This book is dedicated to my father. At the time of publication, he is battling a type of chronic leukemia called Myelofibrosis. He taught me the value behind loyalty, sacrifice, and service. I love you dad, and I strive each day to make you proud.

ACKNOWLEDGEMENTS

Without the unconditional love and faith from my mom, this poetry anthology is not possible. She is the emotional leader in my life, and she keeps me strong.

I would like to extend appreciation to my uncle John, who is a multi-Grammy Award nominee and my greatest mentor throughout my childhood living in San Antonio's Tejano culture. He opened my eyes to the beautiful art of music composition. Musical rhythms and song lyrics ignite the neurons behind my poetry. Thank you John, and my grandfather before him, for shining the light towards that first step through the door of my utmost respect for music artistry.

I want to give thanks to The University of Texas at Austin. The combination of Forty-Acres and surrounding youthful capitol city ignited a creative wonder in my soul. I am extremely blessed to have met people from numerous Texas cities and others with international backgrounds. I carry their founding passions in my spirit. The best part of life is continuing to keep a heart open and learn from each individual opportunity. Education is freedom.

Last but not least, I would like to express the deepest gratitude to those who support and encourage my abilities as a wordsmith. This special knit of friends and family provide me with the spiritual guidance when I need it the most and without a spirited connection, my thoughts and creative nature could not capture amazing moments in this life. This anthology is your homage, for each one of you have a place in these poems.

CONTENTS

Preface	i
POETRY IS THE BEAT OF OUR HEARTS	x
FLASHING REVELATIONS	1
Barbwire Heart (Release Me)	2
Whatever (The Works)	5
Why I Write (My Cure)	7
Character of Truth (My Inauguration)	8
You Did Love	10
My Heart's Petition	12
My Latest Accessory	13
For the First Time, My Last Words Sex, Love, and Faith	14
Seven {Genesis 2:02}	16
P.T.S.D (Poetry Tattoos Saving Dignity)	17
Time to Recover (How Do I?)	20
What It Was, Isn't How It Is Now	22
Heart's on Empty (Deadly Said Rant)	24
Obituary Walls	26
Taking a Toll	28
DREAMS AND DISEASES	31
Dreams and Diseases	32
Trail Blazer	34
My Place	36
Let Me Die (Who Really Knows Me)	38
Her Dead Poet's Dream	40
Tears of Curiosity	42
Known Element	44
This Side Burns	45

I Blame You	47
So Alive in Love After My Dreams	48
Bring Love to Life	50
Romantic Disease	52
History (Write Yours Here)	55
TV Love	57
River Sound	59
Arrows	61
S.T.D. (Sexually Transmitted Demon)	63
A WOMAN'S DANCE	**65**
Only Through Your Eyes	66
World's Dancing Detention	68
A Reminder at My Feet	69
All Eyes on Miss Independent Lover	70
Fallen and Frozen	73
The Heart You Face	74
Night Lie {John 3:20}	77
Rally for Life (A Missing Spirit)	79
Last One I Had	81
Ex Girl	83
Y.S.N.F (Young Sexy Nights Forever)	85
Make Love Freely	87
Heaven Began, Love Again	89
Go Around	90
Butterfly Blessings	92
Rocking Chair	94
Faith and Time as One	96
Love Chamber, You Never	97
Lone Star Ice (Fallen and Frozen Part II)	99
Happiness EXist	101
A Man This Mad	103
Tape	104
Playground Days (Revelry Child)	105
Finally Speak	108

DADDY'S SCARS AND FAMILY   111

Hotel Home   112
Daddy's Scars All Alone   114
Trade Songs Like Tears   116
He Walks Unknown (Father Where Are You?)   118
Face of Place(s)   120
The Hands Memory Left Clocks Dying   122
Closing Wound   125
Whispers of Roses   127
Child Don't Cry   128
A Dawning Love, San Antonio to Austin   130
A Tribute From This Root   132
Some Sad Song   135
Receipt   138
Tickin' Tears   141
What You Face   143

HOW WE LIVE: A WORLD'S WAR   145

How We Live   146
Our Only One Moment   147
Thoughtful Moments   149
The Voice Continues on Broken Records   150
What Did I Miss   154
Back words   156
Existing to Fight   157
This On?   158
Eyes Write a Child's War   159
The Life in a Kill   160
Breathe with Me   163
Verse   164
Suicide Car   165
Watch   168
Screaming Peace   169
No Surprise Attack (United Speech of Infamy)   171

Upon Us	175
Turn of the Ball (Your World, Your Court)	178
Want and Want (Your Attitude, Your Disease)	181
When Heaven Cries	183

SUNSET GENTLEMAN — 185

Left to Dry	186
Eyes to the Sky	188
Put to Death, My Mystery {Daniel 2:03}	189
Angel Flash	191
Some Forgiven	192
Vacuum	194
Call a Friend	196
Bridge	197
A Strike Out Loud (The Last Thunder)	198
Made Of	199
Fire Fighter	201
Hot Glue Gun	202
Love Finds	203
As Long As	204
Coloring the Crush of Love (The Story)	205
What Life Meant	206
Sunset Gentleman	208
In a Heartbeat	211

i.l.a: INSPIRING LOVE'S APSIS — 213

Weekend Made	214
Couldn't Let Her Stay	215
Four Songs (2 Hearts, 2 Worlds)	216
Are You Right Here?	217
Florescence	218
Invisible Love, My Sunset Sweetheart	219
Uncanny (Dreaming Until Our World is One)	221
Love Trapped (Home By Sin)	222
Without Touch	223

Without Touch Part II	224
I	226
I Want to Know	228
As Long As It Takes (Taking Flight)	230
Weekend Made Part II	231
Morning Eyes	233
What's the Matter?	234
In This Waiting Room (ila-Heart)	236
Her Precipitating Mind	237
Whispering Droplets to Ashes in the Wondering Sky	239
In Every Desperation	240
International War Memoir	242
Who Will Tell Me (Close Your Eyes)	243
If Love	245
She Is	247

Preface

In today's information age, I believe the online social network platform is becoming solely responsible for composing an individual's self-esteem and self-discovery. Regardless of the choice in device for Internet connectivity, an individual tends to create and/or destroy his or her emotions, physical appearance, and overall self-identity by the gathering thoughts in every day digital media acquaintances. Attempting to differentiate an online interacting personality from an in-person experience establishes a sense of unintentional fakeness and superficial tendencies where we anxiously change our individual state of mind and behaviors to feel welcome in a world of another personality. Most of our human composition is based on the awareness of emotions, the constructive ideas of others, and the knowledge we develop between the two of them. It is essential to fully understand and express our innermost thoughts in comparison with other individuals, as these become our basic surviving needs to maintain a mutual peace and lay a foundation for a universal knowledge absent of fear and manipulation.

A basic surviving need encompasses the new 21st century self-identity of both online interaction and in-person behaviors. Whether online or in-person, I believe individuals do not feel or understand either interaction fully if they are out of touch with their emotions and if they decide to completely deny who and what drives them. While plenty of self-respect, self-dignity, and self-discovery can come from experience in basic education, such as math, science, history, and nutrition, I believe a person's true admirations should come from how an individual manages and empowers a life event and its occurring (or reoccurring) emotions. These lasting admirations will come from how an individual showcases their predicaments either through written or oral form. Specifically, I have found the art of writing provides a society worthy lessons during turbulent times, and when this art comes to life, it maintains a diverse and unselfish power to help connect the thoughts of one another. By understanding a rapid mental change in any given online or in-person circumstance, these artists ignite a rare and permanent sense of progressive knowledge to share with the world. Further, with this awareness, everything else becomes materialistic, unnecessary, and replaceable. What is irreplaceable and owning is our individual feelings described through written thoughts, for how we exchange this information can power each other's emotional behaviors to either lose control, maintain stability, or to manage healthy growth and change between the two.

What do we owe ourselves outside online profile platforms now and long after the digital age? It will be quite a dare to let go of online social networking when millions of people depend on each digital movement and the new virtual self-identifying perception it establishes. To see all we are capable of accomplishing, as individuals we must be open to letting go of the online status quo. Part of letting go is not about an individual's pace of racing something or someone. Part of letting go is measured by what a person is currently doing to achieve peace for an environment. Time passes quickly and the online social networking age will fade in boredom; however, the compassionate handful of reactions an individual leaves in-person will stay in spirit forever. These feelings will shape the time after the digital age is over. Written personal criticism, both constructive and destruction, will dare to come for who they think a person is or who they desire he or she to be, but endurance defines how a person's attitude and an individual spirit carries toward to an unknown time. We are transcendent, so most problems do not have an immediate known cure, and letting life happen by giving new and abnormal things a chance makes life both challenging and fulfilling. Most importantly, this courage is a reminder that we are alive and we can progress. We must take risks on what is not known and share its outcome appropriately. After all, moral character is truly tested when risks are lived outside securities.

The real self is changing faster than how an individual displays an update for an online social platform, often through unawareness beyond choice. Unawareness is a part of what we are becoming, and frequently it is developed in authenticating faithful ways. We will have failures that do not make it on to an online profile or news feed, and mistakes become instantly displaced in a world's unawareness. Errors go on because an individual refuses to understand the cause for why they exist and therefore, there is not a correction made. In other instances, errors go on because they are purely unnoticed. Consequently, negative aspects may not always progress into success, and if together we do not comprehend the reason for failure, we will continue to make the same mistakes and experience repetitive failures for humanity. In essence, we cannot be afraid to welcome change, whether change is initiated by our general lack of awareness or by the self's desired motive to finally acknowledge when a status quo online age is dysfunctional. Change is an act of doing, and the only proof of this change comes from individual internal thoughts and how we turn theses thoughts into in-person reactions to better communicate with colleagues, family, and friends. To welcome this proof and to evade any such isolation, our self-esteem has to be based on the complete identity of our individual involvement with the world, and with awareness of this mutual identity, either we find creation or destruction in personal authentication.

We compare and contrast what our world is offering to us and what we can offer to it through the medium of online profile representation. Today's instant social network media, televised propaganda, materialistic possessions, and highly profiled lifestyles involving power and control govern the overwhelming status of defining success. Based on whether our success does or does not match the styles in a highly praised celebrity type of pop culture, we frequently create anxiety for a justified individual presence on earth. *Facebook, Twitter, LinkedIn, Instagram,* and our immediate friends and family in a preferred social platform help establish a sense of presence on earth, a common ground with the rest of our everyday in-person relationships. We can compare a status, pictures, and revolving human interactions that fuel an assurance in a feeling of an equalized playing field. In one click, we are as humanly important as a friend, an acquaintance, or favorite celebrity in another profile or webpage. Clicks make us un-alone in our experiences. In one click, we establish a better revealing online personality. In a final analysis it is important to ask, does an individual compare himself or herself to their colleagues, friends, and family (everyday interacting environment), to public figures and celebrities (global environment), or both? How justifiable is it to depend on an online platform each day, and what will be the motivating outcomes?

During a person's life, there will be a common comparable variance highlighting the balanced changes for personal dimensions. Amongst these changes, I believe the most important part miscommunicated and not understood is personal feelings. We are thinking regularly, and as much as we find a link on a type of online social platform, rarely do we organize and credit thoughts verbally and on ink. An online social profile contributes to the endless possibilities of taking a picture and posting it with few words for everyone to view. Accordingly, our innermost emotions disappear without a given chance to be a part of an external self and stoned in written formats. When we refuse to share individual feelings inside a digital world, there are stories untold and a person becomes only a picture. Our pictures in digital media appear to be unfolding a story but without elaborate and rational words expressed, there is a strange perception occurring. This strange occurrence is a 21st century new type of perception we must address. How can we be certain we feel the same emotions of another person if they are rarely revealed? For example, together in a social network picture and through physical contact any one person can pretend to fit in out of the need for acceptance and comfort, but where do true unshared thoughts that beg the opposite emotions find themselves?

What takes over our each individual body is a collective egocentric predicament, the civil war between thoughts, emotional reactions, physical worth, and their collective status of place in the world. The civil war between an individual's validation of his or her online profile and the standalone offline self-worth is the determining factor for understanding a 21st century new human purpose of existence. Once again, *Facebook, Twitter, Instagram* and *LinkedIn* as analogies are my prime examples. In a single picture or for a status update, we seek a collection of positive comments, music lyrics, people quotes, and other influential signs to help mold an identity. In seconds, we are enabled to publish and share anything, truthful and unfaithful characteristics, giving us an ever so desired social status. These constantly changing digital personalities let us create a form of celebrity, because what seems local and close to the heart and mind is able to spread around the world on the same platform in the way that best feeds our needs. Inside these online profile platforms we can be who we want to be. Yet outside the 140-character limiting type of digital world, where does the unknown position find itself (or themselves)? Where does the average human story go? How can one take a picture of our thoughts, and most importantly paint our feelings? How are humans tested to let go of those status quo online profile ideas if we are so hungry for living without risk? Again, isn't true freedom being independent from security? Will the online morality of the status quo, which asks us as individuals to merge with an establishment, cause us to lose our individual creativity? As individuals we each will maintain differences, and we will question one another's motives, but this same result causes normality and a common need for compassion. This compassion is a human being instinct we must recognize in each of us. Although they may think it, some people would never tell an individual face-to-face that his or her digital profile is excessively trying too hard to fit in, or he or she is behaving in specific way because their online environment is doing the same. Therefore, a person can be secretly overloaded with the surrounding feeling of fakeness and some unreal events, which inevitably will cause anger. Do we place constraints on our individual thoughts because we fear irritation and mistrust that will lead to a lost and confused emotion of uncertainty? At what point, will such an emotion start to lead in a new hopeful direction of personal accountability? And when we finally accept accountability, what place, person, or platform will be compassionately available to express those experienced emotions?

    I believe engaging in personal accountability is an extension of art. When we exchange our written thoughts and learn to welcome compassionate reactions those thoughts produce, there is a glue that keeps everyone morally connected. In each of us there is fearless innovation waiting, and this innovation starts with recognizing an internal knowledge of self-faith in a person's soul. Experts proclaim the real self is the conscious self, the one people judge based on their perception of an individual's reactions, except there is a more powerful self description infrequently defined, the one people do not know because a person is afraid to stand in a sitting crowd, exposing the dysfunctions of online connectivity. Too often in a quest for validation of an online profile, unintentionally, we dismiss a place for our individual standalone offline self-worth. In this type of chaotic digital age, our society must find and reveal its spiritual leaders. Instinctively, a person's environment conditions him or her to be nervous when trying to add an individual spirit's diversity to the status quo. A person fears the crowd as it automatically decodes his or her past and present behavior, social-economic class, and future ambitions, placing every single attribute into a category. However, the glue, the substance reminding humanity of its unified richness, is a cleansing leadership towards allowing each person's experience a comfortableness by nature, which opens an individual to artistic self-expression powered by an innate thought absent of premature judgment and manipulation. A society must count on self-expression to create a common emotional exchanging place, the only becoming place, to where souls are not troubled to intellectually mate. This unified world is where we welcome full exposure. Neither social-economic status or an online social network profile, nor any type of physical make up and trending style is morally significant. In the reality of this world, people feel free, and with that surviving freedom comes the ever so fragile emotional stability. This freedom link is the initial goal of my testimony. The motiving outcome of this goal eradicates anxiety and remorse, and humans can live released from status quo shackles to understand new capabilities. Furthermore, the artistry component of this link survives beyond the digital age, and it leads to the everlasting creation of perfection on earth. Perfection is not to be defined by an in-person and online physical body. Let perfection be molded by the hearts a person touches. Perfect enables fearless individuals of every ethnicity, languages, and religions to want to detail their imperfections and uncertainty without judgment or persecution. These absolute results will challenge the 21st century online population and be a cause for implementation. No longer do we have to force tolerance of living in a chaotic technology and rather, we feel the truth in unconditional love in the ways we choose. In this new world, hearts and minds are changed, shared and known, respectively, rather than hand cuffed to the thinking of how physically a person can omit or add to the best description of his or her individual online self for another person's certain perceived liking. Essentially, truth is released time and time again, and most importantly, strenuous energy is redirected toward more pure lessons. Life's truest lesson is not to be afraid or hesitant to reveal what an individual dares to expose, because ultimately, revealing will be the reason for healing.

From birth we are blessed with this seed we should

offer to a world. Unfortunately, most of the time the seed's revealing disappears to an unrecognized place, and we are gone from reality before an initial chance at growth. Thankfully, every morning we get another chance for any reason that generates an intimate connection with our individual soul and those we physically come across. This blossom of expression will leave an overall unbreakable and un-questionable relationship with those individuals who walk with you toward an eternal life. As human beings we must never forget we are given a quest in birth, and although time will have each of us gone from earth, the thoughtful lessons in between will leave an exchanging idea for those individuals who come after to build on.

Nevertheless, I find healing in self-expressed thoughts, both negative and positive, coming from those who are brave enough to detail their life experiences by face-to-face interaction and in written connections. My self-identity, self-esteem, and self-discovery is composed of 1) external essentials, those people willing to exchange emotion, 2) understanding my emotions, which give worthiness to my life's failures and successes, 3) empathizing with another person's feelings and applying them with my own, and 4) what comes with reliving memories. Above all, I know transcendence causes answers to persistently change, but let's never question to recognize the compassion within, the willingness to formulate an action for the greater need of mankind. Compassionate reaction is our enduring motivation for securing universal progressive accomplishment. Mankind is not simply defined by the most famous human beings covered in mainstream outlets. Mankind will be defined as all human beings, of every origin, actively working together through each physical movement to capture true freedom.

*I shall be telling this with a sigh
Somewhere ages and ages hence:
Two roads diverged in a wood, and I—
I took the one less traveled by,
And that has made all the difference.*

- Robert Frost

AN INTRODUCTION
POETRY IS THE BEAT OF OUR HEARTS

There is an inspiring poetry power and saving arts speech describing Robert Frost for the way he saw poetry "as the means of saving power from itself. When power leads men towards arrogance, poetry reminds him of his limitations. When power narrows the areas of man's concern, poetry reminds him of the richness and diversity of his existence. When power corrupts, poetry cleanses. For art establishes the basic human truth which must serve as the touchstone of our judgment." Poetry can be a timeline for an individual's source of emotional destruction and recreation. Poetry can reveal the strength and weakness in a society, whether by an external social-economic way (i.e. theatre, music, dance, etc.) or an internal psychological remedy (i.e. counseling, therapy, medicine, etc.).

Poetry is my self-maintaining emotional thermostat. I have over twenty-five thousand words of poetry, an anthology of more than a hundred and twenty-five poems written in a span of a decade. Each poem was crafted and completed in twenty-five minutes or less. Tallying my human mind relationship through instant feelings and producing reactions, each poem's individual line, title, and theme gives a precise emotional status of what I felt, whom I felt it with, where I was, and where I want to go. I did not rely on mainstream journalism, dubious online social network views, or political propaganda to steer my energy in directions of how I should feel or where I should go from a set of world scenes. Whether in events shared with schoolteachers, colleagues, friends, and family, or in lone experiences, both have revealed lack of awareness into an authenticating transcendental type of self-discovering spirit for me. My spirit began forming into visible literature. What was kept internal had now begun to take its presence on this earth with any individual I chose to share it with. When I first found my spirit, this is what wrote, "I think I ran today, ran with a feeling that I knew could last forever. My heart crashed, it couldn't keep up, and I had to stop. Somehow my body knew you were around, and my mind didn't know where I was. All my worries were gone, and at the same time, I wondered if there was a name for this?"

In the early beginning of childhood, I learned many new things about the world, from feeling the rocks and sand on the playground, to learning the strings and ties of a shoe. While in those recess days as an elementary school child, I was proud to figure out how to tie loose shoestrings awhile recklessly running around and implanting myself in any unknown environment. I did not know where I was going early on in childhood and how I would get there, but I knew the basis for starting to move. Today, this founding idea seems to impact more than my physical movements but also, the circulating mental capacity I struggle to explain in my mind. The basic reading and writing purposes of poetic philosophy are able to spring my uncontrolled thoughts into knowledgeable and mature instincts. These instincts teach how to properly engage in conversations and predicaments by reflecting on all sides of any physical or mental matter and how constructive it is to put myself in other people's shoes of different attitudes and beliefs belonging to a culture. This compassionate learning comes directly from dimensions in poetry.

Poetry has helped me make significant progress in exploring how to respond collectively, responsibly, and elaborately to rising global terror, online networking, and local in-person heart-felt issues. Whether it is *Facebook*, *Twitter*, *LinkedIn* and *Instagram* posts, headline news, sport and music entertainment, or friend and family situations, by developing my morals and attitudes into a movement and a founding philosophy, questions and answers are better understood when I speak and write. Instead of physically tying shoes, I am tying detailed emotional evidence and societal premises to articulate a newer place for exchanging ideas. Consequently, with poetry writing, I am creating rationale, creditability, and endurance for past and present behaviors. This art enables my mind to ease strenuous energy of the long-term nature of a life's time and it points to a prognosis of mankind's evolving purpose for existence day by day. I am learning to engage in more faith by organizing the outcome and meaning behind my favorite activities and passions. Each day is a meaning, from the gasp of an individual's first breath, to the nature of his or her career work, to what baby steps he or she takes to get there. Life composes a digressing, an overcoming catastrophic pause, and progressing type of self-identity. Whether it is because I was automatically placed into a family's traditions, or whether I use part of that entity to create the rest of a life's destiny, my ways of life are repeatedly discovered. Although expressing ideas can be often problematic, scattered, and maintain multi-level depths through a variety of societal scopes, it is my deepest belief that with the application of balancing poetic cores our society can learn to establish healthy and progressive solutions. In this quickly changing digital world, we all do not see the same picture with the same beliefs; however if I step into the mind of another person or their situational self-expressing poetic language, overcast thoughts that we may have can promote and be the reason to predict clearer skies in my mind and in theirs. If there is one lesson given, it is that our most powerful method of currency is thinking out loud with each other through the smallest poetic cores.

  Every day I live with a starving passion for poetic movements, specifically music lyricists and past public figures who relate words to what my eyes and soul hold thoughts to be true. Throughout my days in middle school education, I felt a sense of responsibility to read and write about autobiographies, biographies, and any sort of creative documentaries. What continued to interest my non-fiction addiction the most were the past individuals who shaped our world. These people built the current time that we live in now. For the longest time I did not know how interdependent life truly is. Initially, maybe I denied the understanding of dreams, diseases, death, conflicts, and romance, because I did not want to know the existence of fear and betrayal. However, reading and writing about such subjects open my eyes to unknown things, and this newfound knowledge continues to assist me in differentiating the importance of love, faith, and peace of mind. As selfish and ignorant as we can be, no one person alone can turn failure into accomplishment. In any struggle, whether understanding a diplomatic world hardship, such as trying to stop the exercise of nuclear warheads, or overcoming the crises for family members, like my father who survived a paralyzing 1988 Army helicopter training mission crash and my uncle who died in the Vietnam War at the age of twenty-one, I have learned it is too easy to create by the means of destroying, forgetting the consequences of future days and generations. Weapons, as big as warheads or as small as a fist, manufacture fear, and they are tools inline for mass destruction. Weapons in war rarely create and when used, it becomes an absolute fact for violence and its reciprocation, and whether intentionally or unintentionally provoked, aggression will be born and recycled. Let us always remember unconditional love and intimate faith is what grows and creates. I see water, one of the most natural substances on earth, as the best analogy because with water and patience any flower's seed can rightfully grow under a fractional amount of sunlight. My favorite spiritual leader in the 1960s era said it best, "We all breathe the same air. We all cherish our children's future." At the root of our society's seed will forever be a child who in time will have his and her turns to shape a world for their children. We must ask ourselves each day what kind of prosperity do we want to pass a child? The words we read, write, and speak must turn feeling of inspiration into healthy reactions to stop the fights and corrupting struggles of humanity. Throughout mankind's toughest days, we must think where we begin to lose ourselves in status quo morals and where we can start to find a decent individual identity.

As much as I dedicate my poetic core to colleagues, family, and friends, truthfully, I will never know their perception towards my reactions and my character, which after all these years I had to fight long and hard to capture the most admirable and dignified traits. I remember as a sixteen year old crying and crying over a catastrophic end to a relationship with my first girlfriend, who I had been with for approximately two years. I experienced individual emotional turbulence for the first time. Further, during this time of beginning heartbreak recovery, I learned of spinal degenerative disease that contributed to two herniated discs with excruciating nerve pain in my body. I struggled each and every moment to find love and faith for my self-esteem. Time stood still in tears, trying to figure out how and what I felt inside my mind and fragile unrecognized soul. Easily said, I did not think any one person could relate to my pain. I felt there was no time to listen to the experiences of my immediate family and friend environment, because I needed a speedy cure. I focused on outside forces that sold me love through fear, and I ignored those who always had faith and love waiting for me. I tried to grow up too fast without knowing it, I did not let my cocoon finish the transformation, and I wanted to fly or come out in a quick second, skipping valuable steps that innately I needed so bad. When I look back, was I born broken or simply misinformed, and what initial symptoms and feelings did I neglect all together? We live in a new media civilization that obtains its entertainment by a limited amount of artists and actors who sell love, peace, and security through many solutions of fear and violence. This big business entertainment is transmitted every day on online social networks, television episodes, movie theatres, music videos, and radio stations. Very few stories are told in schools, churches, or by our immediate neighbors. Where does the average human story go? Our stories begin with our guardians. Outside the attention of our schoolteachers, friends, and extended family, we feel the deepest love from mom and dad, and in most instances, we are literally born from a hanging out, cheating, hookin' up, and a first dance sort of thing. Children often believe they are the product of a committed couple. As a child, I was fearful not to be beside them non-stop, next to their unified love during the high emotional periods. A child begins to idealize and mimic the relationships he or she sees, the intimacy in anger and rescuing for happiness, while growing up later to experience personalities of instant Internet platforms. Unfortunately, a growing experiment comes at the determinants of voices, faces, and physiques in most musical, theatrical, and news outlets propagandizing a standard desire to feel love. However, at what age and in what platform will a child become educated in genuine relationships and the fundamental code of respect and devotion?

In these last ten years, from that point in time of my first individual emotional turbulence, I have learned there are a million different equations to equal a loving nature. Those equations provide answers to our everyday education and produce a desire to feel accepted through the formation of true love and faith. There are genuine lessons we never know we give to one another, and inadvertently, we will take teachings from those around us. As quick as time passes, sometimes just showing up, giving the chance for colleagues, friends, and family to physically see you (regardless of how you are feeling that specific day) ignites blissful feelings for others when you are there and later for them to keep your memory when you are not there. Voices and places shared may disappear from our instant mental capacity, but hearing that person again, reading what he or she wrote, or replaying that certain song, enables us to relive those moments we thought we lost. Pictures will always be precious and desperate to remind us of how fun or sad a moment was. When we actually express our written feelings during those slides show images, then that poetic-photo combination will be equivalent to the beat of our hearts. Those beats, that savior pressure of both good and bad emotions rushing to our hearts, are un-dying and remind us how fragile time is. Time is preserved in a smile, a laugh, a kiss, a frown, and a tear, which frequently hold reminder in a journey of a wrinkle. When expressed in written ink, you can put time in your pocket, on your wrist, up on a shelf, or save it and use it when you want to. Time is a refreshing strength exercise that releases unrivaled endorphins. Time can put that favorite color of make up while slipping on those high heels. Time becomes knotted in a necktie and dry-cleaned to that suit. But we must remember time should never fake the emotions you feel. Fake emotions are provoked by those mainstream media sources that sell propagandizing entertainment, which tell you how to feel and when to feel it. You can only make time and feelings live on through the compassionate reactions of your life. Time is always on our side, and you can shape it for those who come after you. It is our colleagues, it is our friends, it is our family, and most of all, time expressed in poetry for an entire world to recognize will unfold a photo, it will release a thoughtful lesson, and it will decode what your each individual heartbeat is truly composed of. Without hesitation, those heartbeats around us will share an invitation to discover a new world.

    I cordially welcome you inside mine. Welcome to *Ignite Your Soul, Release Your Mind Vol. 1*.

FLASHING REVELATIONS

Barbwire Heart (Release Me)

A life came to me today
in red and blue flashing revelations,
the vehicle shape laid undetermined.
I had a right to remain,
or was she at my final rest?
Forever started on the count of never,
here begins the exit test:

My thoughts were never
technologically unwound,
instantly convicted,
and simply jailed,
barred from any freedom.
His incarcerated cyst
promoted catalyst
for the missing and the abused.
They come to me with their hands up,
Welcome to My Prison Camp,
Home of the Hand Cuff Lungs,
there's no key,
no un-locks to find your destiny,
it's as evil inside and out.
Friendly fires don't need to be created,
this kingdom already burning,
as enemies unite with foes,
take a quick listen at what makes
this civil war's cardiac rhythm go.

Oh yes,
I'm sick like a turbulent tumor,
but you're the one skipping beats,
like a remote that fast-forwards
an unforgettable scene.
I must have had
some type of heart murmur,
'cause she choked on things
I shouldn't have told her.

Look, she suffocated
but I'm the reason she's alive,
I'm the Chris Brown,
and she can thank me now.
I hit you with some sense
from your mistaken innocent breath.
I can't say I don't give a ….,
I can't say I'll do anything, but
I did lay down a life so you can live yours.

Who knows what it is to be saved?
How confined concentration is?
Something only shown down this vertebra,
as squeezing bones prosecuted a nerve,
like her beauty,
most numbing injuries were undefined.

She didn't feel her worth
until his sun struck her eye.
He has seen the pain is one in the same,
not something he couldn't diagnose,
he simply had to rename.
I know my judgment,
its blindness
is a tendency.

She jumped the gun like running
without her high-heeled shoes,
he knew it's going to hurt
once she hit those heated roads.
Baby, do that desert dance,
a happily ever after ripening romance,
and don't you ever count on a bloody past!

My love is like a barbwire,
once you jump,
you will collapse,
once you get cut,
it regenerates a heal,
the time when there's a wrong

stitched in your tissue's seal.

Forbidden climbs aren't so fearful
once you find a pathogen,
it's like that reoccurring dream
with buried defensive hearts
turning its casket into life.
The inevitable
and the use to be haunting,
now ever so touching,
let my heart's neurowires
be recovering wounds
that finally take down that fence,
where you can supply a reborn cell again,
where permanent scars are today's wisdom,
life's sentences.
A new world,
all is here to vent,
like we're pitched under a global verbal tent,
where you release that one mistake
to have new air like a repairing stent.

Whatever (The Works)

Forgive them father
for they know not what they do;
it will be right or literally dead wrong,
my thinking is becoming uncontrollable.

They say what I have is an excuse,
but it will have a truth for a use,
like a needed light for the fuse.
The fireworks and whatever works,
the cigarette and the cancer,
for the kingdom they set on fire.

Sometimes the beginning
is what the end demands,
for the rest of my life
we're born quickly dying,
but darkness doesn't mean I'm dead,
it's a surrender to survive.

Other times a team needs change,
like a different and new player
in the same game.
The battlefield will be the air I breathe
with no rivalry,
as long as it's there
my mouth can't run out of words.
This poetic justice is my language
for when society doesn't have one that works.

If you can't adjust
and don't see what I speak,
wait for flash,
the flame will come in
like blood shred after you realize the heart has a leak.
This is my heart attack,
my pronoun,
for when love strikes,
this is how it will sound.

The show,
like after an ignite
for cannon ball works,
and when a global sky
finally gets
the entertainment she deserves.

Why I Write (My Cure)

Struck of the artery,
struck of the brain's nerves,
who will wish
they recorded a few words?
When the AED beeps a straight line,
when they cut to save your life,
done can always be undone.

Look back to the thought of
a rough draft,
it leads the dead.
Write another
and feel the air to love another.
When there is only one life to give,
desperation is all we have to live,
like an emergency to 911,
make a call to those you love.
It's only one finger
in the press of send or that pen,
open up to the world
before that final pulse
is uncontrolled under the knife.

Point the index at this:
You don't have to be a cardiac surgeon
to mend the heart,
only know a spirit lies
where the ink and mind begin.
Prefer to bypass
the write in your words,
then voice all your concerns.
Speak in vain
or speak to save a vein,
stress will release,
a life can be saved,
and the cycle beat,
for cure is in the hand,
subsidizing any disease.

Character of Truth (My Inauguration)

Where does life begin
and where does end?
You wouldn't believe me if I told you.
It lies in the collapse of a soul,
praying to release the truth,
when a confuse mind begins to excuse,
for in an illusion you find
what you really want to say and do.

I wonder who I am now,
when involuntarily I fell into you
routinely sunrise to sunset.
You lived the blame
awhile we directed the make of love,
oh how we risked years of reward and regret.
You are my miracle,
but I can no longer think about you twice,
I'll write my fate here,
hoping you can evacuate the mind.

When eyes open,
I cry to the Lord,
I can't take how you only come to life at night.
I bury the pictures,
but she finds her way to be sent through space,
as distance becomes further,
dreams keep you secret safe.
If this is where I have to be
and while leaving my history
in an isolated city,
this is my new beginning.

Sometimes unfamiliar territory fits
because what we already know will hurt.
I can't hide from what is done,
who I am,
and who you aren't,
although my contentment

glorifies her goodbye,
we must go ahead
with broken swears left behind.
We force inauguration
when lies have been told,
and current hands of time let the past hold.
Whether intoxicated
in hopes of eliminating the taste of her lips,
or recalling her love in my cries of sobriety,
her memories begin and end your discovery.

I'll tell any friend to love like she is dying.
Lean on an open heart
at moments of disorientation
because in the waves of collision,
her mirror will be as immense
as an oceanic reflection.
And for those who
remember me and you,
crisis will capture
our character of truth.

You Did Love

You know you held the key,
that's why I'm lying at the door
pleading mercy.
You did love,
and I didn't show you enough,
I swear I was wrong strip of all-purpose.
Was it worth it?

Only time will tell.

I'm content I can turn this over,
oh Lord, mend this heart to be a lover.
In one trip into the fall,
I thought we been through it all,
now we are ending?

Into December,
I remember,
how could this be?
I beg for a new beginning,
oh baby it's cold,
my blood can't compete,
I feel it down the body
as these bones become weak.
I stare at the clock,
its shade reminds me of you,
you did love,
and I wish your hands would go back.
Maybe the shattered mirror
will now learn,
we live forth faceless,
counting on peace to joint this heart piece.

The world chaotically
continues to turn, and
moon light orbits me confused,
while the rays of sun
shred our happy moods.

So I guess we will stay
sightless to the I love yous.

Friends by day,
foes by night,
lonely silhouettes
become all we know to figure
a common ground,
the only force left never to unite.

By land, as high as we want to fly
our feet can't leave this surface,
and while sailing amongst the water,
the weight of my soul is kept anchored
at the depth of the sea,
no waves, no air,
nothing moves you to see
what I believe.

You did love,
and one day
I will grow out of your shadow.
Maybe now or maybe never,
these words could once again
beat the sound of your heart,
goodbye to the next welcoming days of your life
as you part.

My Heart's Petition

Don't question,
you never had to question,
my hearts petition to love you
line by line,
because this song will do
my love for you right.

You can say I will cheat.
The war we lived laid two sides in defeat.

I stand still in this room
for you to undo this kill.

Giving in meant
not wanting to win,
because losing you
would be no victory.

Sleeping in your unshared doubts,
left lifeless here by your question,
your uncertainty.

You moved,
I'm stuck
housing these reminisces of you,
when I said love,
it is the only truth.

My Latest Accessory

Where do you want it to be written?
Crying to world
but there's no complement in our day,
you assert your heart remains voiceless
because of the things I say.
The crime I've committed,
striping you of your skin,
cold as you lie,
weak from bone to bone,
circular motion we go, alone.

Declare war in the stare of our eyes,
suffocating lungs
and bodies held warrantless.
I carry you on my sleeve,
no further,
again breathless,
some word short of "I love you"
becomes too far to catch.

When I'm on my hands and knees,
when I'm begging please,
you call,
"This time is final,
kiss me before you miss me,
today, I can't live dialing denial."
Through all the photos,
the X's and O's,
one sentence detains a soul indefinitely.
While you will always shock a heart's statute,
I say, "Farewell my accessory."

For the First Time, My Last Words Sex, Love, and Faith

Death to one,
lit resurrection to two,
let my restraint prove it to you.

You said things will stay the same
and yet baby so much has change.
If I was an addict,
maybe you had some kind of insecurity,
a part you wanted to fill,
pleasure in pain
the ride you loved to kill.
There had to be more to us
than lust in the making.
Faith rising to love,
a trip that bent the cell far enough.

We escaped,
we escaped!

Running away from each other,
still so many moments an unknown
God tries to relapse a save.
Why won't selfishness ever go away?

The last words I said,
can I please have a couple back,
or did I not say anything at all?
How could you have ignored a call?

In that dying moment,
if I laid you down
when you said kiss me now,
how would that continue to sound?

Waiting too late not wanting to know,
now, these stolen songs
follow me everywhere I go;

Whispering walls of freedom,
eclipse of a new feeling in every room,
doors that refuse to be locked,
the flood in the paint
that holds a blockade of love.

How am I suppose to release
the only emotion I'll ever know,
shut off the playlist to a sleeping silence,
hoping to shatter the shadow?

You don't lie when you cry,
I think these tears
will define the rest of my life.
When I was too young to recall,
baptism wet dream
didn't need a sound to save my soul,
no matter how loud it gets,
worship does control.

Nailed to forgiveness,
let the last words be my only witness:
Resurrection as a new direction,
point good deeds that haunt to an inner peace,
remembering a love sacrificed can never leave.

Seven {Genesis 2:02}

The truth began on the seventh day
as two inadvertent hooks caught revelation,
shame on me for this temptation.

Beaten by wisdom,
I crash confession
when our skin screamed
producing all that is evil.

Rushing, swinging,
loving sounds so loud,
drowning repetitively in the same cloud.
The last time kept hurt at rewind,
holding on to emptiness in fanatic fashion,
dislocated side by side,
beyond control,
lying by your eyes made broken years whole.
Oh how you spoke with silence,
but still I never gone this long.
Where is the ambulance?

I lost me in a poetic peace
on the unsung first day,
now I'm begging for yesterday.
Until angels messaged me,
"God is our maker,
time is our taker,
no matter the faults,
earthquakes will turn into needed breaks,
and when it rains,
let it pour 'cause spirits will still soar."
I dared to fall and I did,
survived in the latter,
finding these precious pieces
and still I gather.

P.T.S.D (Poetry Tattoos Saving Dignity)

Modern day ideogrammic
selling Ezra by the pound,
he didn't distribute Molly,
he sculpts a common Frost,
a detail in the fabric
like Mraz's song for the lost.
They called him the playground child
in jungle gyms around a tatted poetry palace,
roses pulled
and sneakin' ways to plant the climb
from ungodly dates,
learning ink of international queens
on their new MacBook word plates.

She hit a Google map,
okay study time over,
"Can I come over?"
He said it's time,
he brought the college shame,
and she told,
"I can be the reason
for loaning one night rent."
Heads or tails?
Let's flip the JFK fifty-cent piece,
no half way there doors,
close it fully baby.
It was something repugnant
to hear foreseen roommate drama,
he only hoped that he could be forgiven
and wanted from drug sheets trauma.
Missed calls, and return texts,
no sleep after sixth,
skeletons in and out a poetry palace,
high heels done on the laminate floor,
one too many bedskins lay there beautifully to unlace.

The truth is
they did him like a Twitter tweet,

in the morning,
a reminder for love suicide,
all too drunk to realize
the crushed friendship later.

Until it started again,
one moment
he was checking the ageless rhythm
of a harmless sex ledger,
the next, he died an overdosed joker
like Heath Ledger.
Face painted and frozen
in a reflecting glass of Seagram ice,
those addicting Austin street nights,
what do you know
about bingeing for venoms of lust signs?

First kiss in hallways,
on innocent cheeks falling,
then a face disappeared below,
and all of a sudden,
consulting a girl with the texting tears of trust.
What do you know
about guilty taxi rides?
Young sexy birds changing clothes
to release skin smoothness,
block phones and batteries
dying like consciousness.

The freedom in her body,
she held him up
like a robber stick up,
crimes locked in
a brain wave
for far too long,
every lesson laid in time
as his eyes saw
generation dresses become shorter,
and he let her become a mean taker.

She had no recollection
of what she did to him
with every girl after,
her trigger carried his name
for a new age sinner.

Before, his lungs wrapped
the space so sweet,
until she placed a tripwire
at every crack of his soul,
his walks were busted tears,
and when he tried to run,
his disease recreated
passionate nightfall flashbacks.

He would never be
what women wanted from him,
he kept flipping that coin,
on his own love suicide,
living in his mind
from new apartment room,
reminiscing doom
in every tattooed poetry palace

Time to Recover (How Do I?)

Time to recover in this lonely hour,
more than the need for protein,
more than the aftershock of you and me,
let this single title be
the feeling in a heart's frequency.

Seconds will continue second-guessing
the fight of a fractured mistake,
once you win it and begin an abuse to lose,
all my quitters and takers
start reading here looking for a fuse.
I don't blame you
when you say promises do not exist
judging by questionable memories that persist,
let this be a prayer in a fearless manifest.

We can change you and me,
the temperature room-to-room,
once you step out of your mind
and into mine.
So when I'm climbing
and begging to hold on,
this is the only thing I'll keep in the inbox
trapped inside there's 'still life' box,
where a face of a dream remains mentally locked.
They say photos do not lie
but they don't see
how honest a fictional story can be.
While locking lips
were slowly springing letters,
like a rocking chair back and forth,
pictures caught
only an ounce of a thousand's worth.
From fallin' in
and out of arms of love,
to fallin' in and out of bars,
trying to find
which drink will diagnose

these tender parts.
The more I fill an empty a glass,
the more I see a scenic past,
trailing any perfume scent
ignites a permanent reminisce,
like letters dropping in blood shouting forever,
holding down a "never die"
enlistment of a shiver,
up and down the spine,
through ups and downs of our life.

Who would have thought
your absence could save me every time,
in this brand new mind of how do I?
Who would have thought unforeseen closure
bringing you closer,
granting time to recover
like this request for a new age sinner?

What It Was, Isn't How It Is Now

So you're going to crucify me
for my actions that took place long ago,
well, healing takes time to grow.
Yes I was some kind of child living in denial.

I could say sorry,
but I will never win.
I don't want to.
Yes, I hit you,
abused to manipulate.
It was the same actions your father had to take.
There was no answer
until he became sober.
Well so have I!

What it was,
a curse of fate between the two of us?
Down the same bridge, the same track,
no longer do I run in circles,
I pledge to be like one of Jesus' new disciples.
I found my new testament
with only God as my witness,
making a few friends,
hoping the more I do for them
the less they will pretend.
Only two people I come to stay true to,
one gave his life to the skies,
the other was always you!

I hit you in the face,
now, I live with the scars
every time I see the mirror,
my own face.
I can't wipe away the ghost in the glass,
that's me, that's how it has to be,
walk on to carry you in life's suitcase.
Maybe I will continue to trip,
and shoe by shoe,

solely and slowly,
I tie up my lace.
I don't know
where my feet can take this soul,
I pay and pray everyday for the bruises
and how I lost control.
A reflection always had
some magic to lay a new road.
I can ride alone,
a new me to own.

Yes my bad, my faults,
I created the crack
by a self-inflected deep impact,
and I still swing each hand,
not at you,
throw them up
in a new direction,
and back down
with faith in the desert.
Somewhere there has to be water
amongst the sand,
sometimes giving in,
never give up,
like an apostle,
no matter how badly
I think forgiveness seems impossible.

What it was,
isn't what it is now,
choices will have reactions
so inevitable,
somehow stay strong,
only I decide what is invincible.

Heart's on Empty (Deadly Said Rant)

I'm on E.
When you become like me
are we able to see how no one can care?
Mistakes made all in love
and nothing will be fair.
They see me on the road
stranded without an exit,
I was there for her entertainment.
Stare me in the eyes and look,
still I could not face it.
Trip after trip, on the track
I forgot to lace it,
it's like the further you persist
no one claims a love knot to exist.

On E, she's not the one like Billie Jean.
Mile after mile, that one has millions
and millions of reason
why the clock continues to lose its tick,
and here comes the dynamite
with a blaze of the wick.
The more I stay the course,
the more I see the body bag of a peace soldier
and his corpse.

Will reality in love
hit when feelings are dead,
or when she finally speaks
everything I wanted to hear
will be finally said.

That lone voice administers
my last rights on E,
no fight for you
left in me.
Heaven's traffic has me
waiting to die
stuck on a different trail

off the rail.
An E and motion
in life failing to unite,
from land to a terrorizing sea
the same picture I see.
Lakes and oceans can't handle
the overflowing river of a child's cry.
I have the world at a sink into my pocket,
fish undone by any net.
Still not one willing to catch on?

I'm on E,
on this line,
empty,
I have had one too many.
I did what it took,
no one cares
living with all the dirty stares.

Since when have we controlled
the make love?
Now a day, it's more innate to hate
in the power we try to create.
Like trying to manipulate
oxygen off thin air,
and live by CO_2,
forgetting to breathe,
forgetting the you I have in me.
As I turn, I always give you my back
but when I'm comfortable in a casket,
will you still talk behind that?

Dispose of me in the vest of truth,
cry for the bullets
happening to always get threw.
On E is collapsed from being the last
bleeding one out of fuel
with the punishment unusual and cruel.

Obituary Walls

Every wall I turn to constructs
four sides of the heart
I want to hide in.
This is my room
for those who run to me
and run from me.
I'm sitting here staring at the screen
thinking it has the cure,
for all these lights
I have to see something for sure.

It's getting late,
the dark crack of the door
becomes a dizzy earthquake,
waiting for your shadow,
let me look a little bit more,
scrolling,
hoping the answers will appear.
Somehow there's nothing
but misprinted words here.
There's an I, a love,
and a you,
lips, lies, lust
breaking by a ceiling fan
as you always came before I,
again insecurity derailed you in
when you saw another's girls eye.

It was the wrong order,
another story of a long lost
and found revolver.
Some say you ain't worth the roulette shot
when you did me in
like the last screw to the coffin.
I post each obituary up
on the wall as motivation,
for some energy to turn into happiness.
They say everything good

later in my life will be a witness
for how I didn't sex you,
and I wasn't aggressive to touch you.
This is for all the fucks you used
to try to find someone like me,
and you realized it was only me in you,
you wanted to feel.

Better now, sew it up
until your gold conquest is at a heal!
You're damaged.
I'll pray to the sex god
to talk to the last God,
devil versus Jesus,
which is where
your unclothing ways leaves us.
I wanted it slow
to last farther than you and me,
something for a world's children to see.
A model for everything that is forever.

I had plan,
wrote it line by line,
you didn't believe it.
My promise wasn't like a virgin,
I was going to keep it.

Taking a Toll

I'm done creeping hopeless romantic,
I'm going the other way,
I'm experimenting with the devil's toll way.
Until my loan on thoughts make a zillionaire,
I'll accept the charges I don't care,
I'm going to hit you with a collection tax,
profit of my loving lessons,
while you count your blessings,
before a slam to the floor,
I'm like a crumbling skyscraper
that keeps the history and its stories.

I accept I'm abusive,
banging my brain like a piggy bank,
and in your heart that won't stop beating.
I'm running out of values
and you can't catch your breath,
what I use to be, you did not believe.
It's relative in my words,
so I'll say,
"I'm not good at intimacy!"
I get addicted
and a voice is all I will want.
So I pretend
I hear your mouth through my mind,
that's what seems right.
There laid a grave for your knowledge
when you didn't speak it,
a loser in love
like hell's cry never can show it.

I hit the devil's capsule,
hands are locked and waiting implodes,
I wasn't the only begging one,
I'm the dude that tried to have more fun.
No one can predict my tongue,
it's dancing in my casket heart.
I'm alive from the dying

like hide and seek,
only I decide when I want to peek.

If you can't find the relic,
keep scrolling,
keep a listen to the stereo I type.
Forget the net or the press,
new news in my two lips as a dyad,
with them I can guarantee heal,
after I'm done speaking
what you never felt
will make you feel
like you're born to feel.

DREAMS AND DISEASES

Dreams and Diseases

I shared rejection
like the same two sides
in a magnet,
I believed my dream
lied in your disease.
When they said
the pieces wouldn't fit,
like a broken bridge
that wasn't love,
and this wasn't enough,
I made the skull to thick,
the heart became too easy to mold,
and together,
they both lost control.

There was a wait in a game
I was willing to play,
some kind of match
burning in desire
depending on a bed
which stirred up
an indestructible fire.
I hated to breathe
without your lips
resuscitating me,
but we brought alive
what can't be taken back,
you and I found
what we shouldn't have.

We smiled and laughed
at the rod we did cast
from the boat
that could never really stay afloat.
Haunted and crashed by waves
louder than an Japanese quake,
swirling in the brain,
your dream

reminded me of reality's mistake.
A miracle made believable
with deceiving,
wounding wishful thinking.

It did happen,
I choked into hell,
from a disease catching one under a spell.
A dreamt hex and the sex
merged for a rupture,
like a busted soul and its mind
waiting to see a suture.

Trail Blazer

I saw the flame
before I entered the trail
on the road of hopes and dreams
he passed hell.
He said, "Nice to meet you,
but you look familiar."
Most likely in reply,
"I've lived here and there."

My eyes can't seem to escape
what I continue to see,
I'm breaking,
searching for signs to point
to where I want to be.
This drag is lonely; it's all I know,
always separate but the same lead.
Here comes another destination,
that unsophisticated temptation.

She tells me to follow
in my nature of she's not to hold,
quite a dare, lost in her smile,
I'm loving the feature.
Once again he fights denial,
Déjà vu,
I preach to her.
"If you're going to attempt
at my heart,
you better break with it."

Built like a mountain,
I broke along
echoes of hellos and goodbyes,
dealt with a haunting route
surrounded by cries.
Pain, heartaches,
and kisses infect an endless mistake,
where yesterday swallows today

and I digest humble;
Above these useless
maps and photographs,
in a kingdom
promising mine of gold.

Another mumbles,
"I want what you give
but don't trust me in loving you.
Shake the compass
for it's your only truth.
Go on soul shuffle, rattle, roll,
and burn bold,
maybe now love can listen
to what I've told,
intercourse dares to be sexual
'cause they don't know intellectual."
Exposing bodies
instead of stripping the mind,
I combat what I can't save.
Surely I got some sort direction,
faith has to be more
than these blockades of temptation,
in shameless helping hand of a "sex-taint,"
walking on and walking off,
like the next contestant.

My Place

There is a place,
a place where I want to go
and laugh at all I now know,
where forgotten names
ignite a permanent light in the sky
and you can finally
think about me all the time.
A place where a clock
and its hands can't judge
what he took in the past,
where going is always coming
like a revolving door,
a place where surrendered
is actually a win,
while healed at
bleeding wounds of a sin.

Please write the wrongs of my life
in a book that is forever shut
like the mouth of the word
I should have never spoken
and I become forgiven.

I'm lifted sitting on a cloud
watching you,
waiting for all-time wings
to wind a song
in a chance
that can forever be blown,
and heartbreaks are sewn.

The more I sing,
the louder you get,
and I stay
like a statue in one place.
I never have to run nor escape,
you can come visit,
I'll be right here.

I'm not moving
or making promises
only out of happiness,
no cries,
no loving
or remembering
out of fear.

I want to say bye
and put you
in another life,
where you for me
always meets the eye.

Let Me Die (Who Really Knows Me)

Let me die;
let me have
this one moment in time.
I can go before you.
Nothing in life is fair,
it's a fatal game once we're born
we all are forced to play.

Let me die in my one day,
to speak and the world will listen,
to give and I'll receive a hug back,
to believe and it all becomes a fact,
to beg and forgiveness eyes my name.
I want to live like
we never had anything to change,
back to our innocent ways,
back to when music
had a one dance motion,
didn't play with an emotion.

Forget my
what *I know now* policy,
it's too much stress;
If I don't,
who really knows me?

Take me back
to where girls were always friends,
nothing more;
Boys played for pride
'cause nothing was to be won,
it was a game with only fun.
Winning's worth had no value,
it was one code to unlock
a repetitive discoverable world
of me
always finding you.

It was that touch of a hand's transaction,
where laughin' and smilin'
is the only kinetic feelin.'
Take me back to where
a glimpse is engraved
as forever;
Take me to where
memory will be unnecessary
now nor ever.

Her Dead Poet's Dream

It's coming to a close,
I've done an addict to reach
everything what has
in a sky's clothes.
I took a request,
in came something her man
became to regret.

Tell me,
do dead poets dream?

There are times
where I'm diving
in river cracks of forever
and others where
he eclipses her only for a moment,
most days it's up to whom loaned it,
lips bolted in a video
of an enemy's demise of a ex,
bars torching a desk,
dances go live in recorded sheets,
a heart comes down quicker than how
a blind man's eye bleeds.

She never knew
a new age sinner's song,
she never knew
the drink of a father
seemed to script them all.

Woman, woman!

A couple of fingers fire
before anyone saw a call;
Every time she proceeds
in any man's conversation,
he doesn't know I'm there,
he doesn't know

skies' past midnight stare.
Pay attention
to the way moons see;
Listen to curtains coming down
and how she lays.
Shhhh baby,
I guess it's not only us alone.

It's coming to a close,
happiness
belongs to sounds of a button,
the fastener,
a wicked ceiling fan,
the dismantled strap,
and chills running down her back.

Tell me,
do dead poets dream?

Let's replay
a sanctified scene;
Let Dalí paint
reunite what he will feel:
Helen Jane Long pianos
recovering a bed of roses;
Done stealing petals
of an unheard addict,
to whom made skins
fall deeper than
what moons change it.

Tears of Curiosity

I stood in line of one,
waited through all the scenes,
when it felt like
I was the last of a thousand rounds,
I realized that it is only you.
In tears of curiosity,
along the scope of when a man
and a woman first met,
we never knew where
human waterfall eyes start to set.

A woman's hand ignited ecstasy
by the touch of her magnetic phone,
toward our lost wind flew time
in a tongue from crack to crack,
gravitating kisses goodnight
on drifts at a striking meter;
our reborn bay canyons.
Runaways thundered
on foot faster than a stallion
and mercy sounds
tied to a two legged heart.
There I go,
there goes my keyless lock
traveling in a trembling women's flock.
Violins played along as airborne plans,
each string for those I passed in shame,
and his insecurity of trust
rebounded one in the same.
Loving one by one,
two less and deeper alone,
the tears of curiosity
continued my war zone.

Faster and faster
there goes his heart to the sky,
from crawls to footsteps,
to full on sprints,

two Texas cities lightin' up
one too many spirits.
I gave the ounce
to the pound of what my skin felt,
nothing could make her melt.
Too cold, too in disguise on her own,
sometimes going forth has its never,
coming out the cement
of what was suppose to be
the world's unseen flower.
Strings stripped
rose petals of her puppet,
when I can no longer be patched,
I realized that was me
in what I found in you.
All her, so responsive
in what is addicting,
she said,
"I can only promise your last drug."
In this world of one,
she said, "Isn't that enough?"

Every touching hand reminded me
of what a day demanded from a night,
and every ring reminiscent
of a vulture's mapped out direction,
by flowing tears of curiosity
from her turbine lips
landing this heart-abduction.

Known Element

As loud as I dream,
it may never be heard,
so when the moon
and the sun unite,
this is what I write:
Running too long
into your skin of lust
for senseless sin.
I've coped
and I will always bleed,
become one
with this deadly lead.
It's a race
against black and white,
painting old demons
into the eternal night.
What have I lost if I came in alone,
another date in this diary?
I,
then at end of a word
come *u*,
as recycled letters
depict haunted imagery.

Spent your years misguided
and still no,
I don't perplex!
Resorting to peace,
so don't con my text.
A game of gain
with depreciating value,
I run to this element to shield me
from those like you.

This Side Burns

I rise,
the morning's got me night turning,
looking for something
we can no longer see.
This blank has infused combust
or shall I deem a lonely lust.
No familiar face,
only scaring her sheets in
what you can't erase;
She stays with you ultra-violetly,
when the sun burns out,
selfish me stays beyond third degree.

You shouldn't touch
what I can't feel,
whether it's real,
time to survive in
a vexatious peripheral.
Embattled I run
towards any convenient shell,
is this my self-defense
or my self-regress?
With fire in my arms,
I live obsess,
telling me love is
a retroactive weapon,
a war within,
daring to find a depend on.
Addicts we run
manipulating bottle-euphoria,
yelling at him and her,
elated to hear no more of ya.

Angels! Angels!
We all fall down
to your universe
still living in thirst;
All we become

is a blinded burst,
from dusk to dawn,
I will be burning
armed at your invisible side
until justice is done!

I Blame You

I hear your laugh
as chapters disperse,
am I glad you came
or do I still carry a curse?
Although you brought ignorance,
I am the liar,
I gave in to a seducing desire.
Faith laid redundant
as a soul bled dry,
emptied its veins to forget
you and I.

I stand here historically struck,
blaming you for my dismal luck,
bankrupt because for you
I am in debt,
but like when a head hits the pillow,
I'm forever glad we met.

One day I will discover
the keys around this ring,
are they to hearts to fill my own?
Until then,
I walk alone.

So Alive in Love After My Dreams

I woke up this morning,
saying,
"This is it!"
Dead and I've never felt
so alive in after my dreams.
Almost floating above
an ocean of uncertainty,
it became true,
I hit a straight dive
into a breathless pool,
I could no longer be ugly
to anybody,
forgetting that picture
they placed on a face.

Baby, some hope painted you.

Beautiful mistakes were
few days that brushed
and bruised me,
in the roses she left
after she kissed me,
and the bullet shells she left too
when she was gone.

Questions were at the lighthouse
I never had to reach,
wrinkles winded my ageless sail
and some hope broke away
 a world from its leash.
Some type of face operation
at hospital heaven,
it chose me.
It wasn't going to be my exit.
Her face,
my only entrance
for the next plan,
this is the story of a new man.

With a chance,
a like,
and a finally loved,
over and over again,
the fit of the glove
took me by hand,
a kiss,
and a lasting storm,
the hurricane took everyone
but one.

She fell over my mind
at the drop of the wet rosary,
sunk deep into my heart
swirling through this faithful bloodstream.
I told her,
"What a tragedy,
but there's only one way out of this life,
and I'm glad you love me."

I died
when she came
inside my heaven,
my heart;
This is where
my only love life starts.
Let's make war,
make love,
diplomacy
and intimacy,
with the roses ready
and the gun loaded;
Let them all strike,
I know
I'll wake up
to where I want to be
after this world war night.

Bring Love to Life

He's something
like a prophet
in the making,
when she reads
the lyrics to this,
no not the money,
the kind of love
that rains eternally.
She could romanticize
by a flip of pages in a book,
and he can only take one look.

From a crazy dream,
she'll sprinkle words of love,
and he'd find a completed chase
by the letters entering reality,
her wish, his grant,
brings life to you and me.

He could lie
to make you remember his name,
or decide to tell you the truth,
as you cautiously seek more proof.
Ask him to walk further
while in your nodding head,
you wonder
and they begin to discuss,
his eyes, his charm,
her smile, and her laugh,
what's there to lose
between the rumors in the two of us?

She let's go,
like the releasing sound
of a pair of beating clouds
begging to let it rain;
Striking hearts

begin to crash down to the surface;
They say to one another,
"Loving you
is my life's purpose."

You could be her
and he could be me,
although sometimes
love is something
you read and never see,
at sun's first peak,
it's all we need.

Think it to life
then recite
from the pass of
a precipitating note
you thought you could
never feel to write.

Romantic Disease

I can't tell them what it is,
I can only show a secret exposed,
simply for you to know.

They ask does she make you feel bad
or will this feel good?
I wonder myself
if I feel like I could?

I adore this collision,
this is how
I see my life's vision.
This is a sacred part
of the ocean in me,
a magnetic wave of persistent love,
in every fiber to every piece of the bone,
this piercing skin has to be enough.

We could be paper thin,
counterfeit
and live off a bounce of quarter,
toxic you and foolish me
make perfect sense,
no matter the countless shots,
let ecstasy fly,
forget that taste of innocence.

Let time go!

Given hope turns
this nervous tongue into action,
let my hands heal
an all-alone attraction.
Paint you alive in
and out this picture
for a metaphor,
scream, I love you
on the highest floor.

Let me ride this antenna
until it reaches you,
with your thunder
and my conductor,
I dare rise
above the electric mist;
I can't stop,
don't you pull that plug!

When you cry,
I hurt.
We're worth fight.
Stinging the love out of life
and shock life
back into love,
dose by dose,
we take turns
attacking the viral host.
Like a romantic disease,
I'll inject the vaccine,
if you suture my honest bleed.

At the brink,
when they say
we're about to experience defeat,
who are they
to diminish your dream?

When you're ridin',
please promise
a saddle waiting for only me,
and know as you
recite magical new words,
I'll show your heart
must always come first.

Sin will be sin,
forget the apathy,
it can never win.

Spark your smile
and love
is destine to burn;
Remember a fire
is nothing to hold a concern.

This could be natural
or be on a latitude claiming disaster.
You have to believe
for selfless once,
you are the princess
in this happily ever after.

History (Write Yours Here)

Eyes on the broadcast
this is my history,
I write my own,
absent of any conspiracy;
I like to sign off
knowing you didn't forget anything,
over again, it's the title that gets me.
Maybe this is a phase or a lonely chase,
but I won't let her be a mistake.

I could circle this 365 days a year,
I've had, made it,
stood one night
bringing her body no fear.
More than any being
could consume in a lifetime,
God knows
any girl preciously remembers mine.

I tell them where to touch;
On my charm hangs
the string of my heart,
an irresistible language
residing between a lung
that tells me how
you want this story to be sung.

I ride romantic
in decades of disenchanted;
I've been on top
and on the bottom,
laying beside
what I call my world.

Am I over disease now,
or maybe until
I revolve another skin,
or until I find

the inventor of this sexting technology,
most certain I won't be giving
any dream an apology.
Endlessly, I know Romeo and Juliet
will let centuries' plots play.

TV Love

What feeds their electricity?
I deem the drug
on this cable connectivity.
Kill the tube;
blast the channel
in this merry go round,
I beat and beat,
wishing you could write
how love comes down.
Change it to yours truly,
would you do that for me?
Let the pen strike
or wait for the keys to ignite.
Baby I hear the static,
who is destine to fight
what we don't want to see?
I stay blinded when lust
and love is sold
as the same damn thing!

So you want to feel sexy,
when there's more cleavage than brain?
She has sticks in her shoes
so she finally can't run,
who are you
when the make up is gone?
Not saying your phony
but something more is at stake.
You think it has to be gross for him
to get off to plastic,
oh how a cancer patient
would enjoy those hair extensions!

Your screen's infected too,
not content,
there's some lifestyle disconnect.
Once you've seen
the flame in a shot glass,

you instantly
and externally undress.
The bed and you bare
is unbearable,
as she forgets what's inside.
I promise
once you open the door,
there's more.

Let me help you
with that trigger
you're about to pull,
press this button,
turn off the TV,
shred the magazines,
stop trying to click on celebrity.
Baby, you got all
Of that woman's beauty
and more, let's move
in permanent fashion.
Retro reciprocated,
we aren't turning back,
it's what you always had;
the most liberated accessory.

Spread the word,
I'm releasing hearts,
one for your sleeve,
one for your enemy,
no diamonds, no gold,
no fine print to be told.

River Sound

I am the river
that flows through your head.
I'll put the gun to your ear,
now what was it that I said?

The water is your wires
feeding you what you deserve.
Blame yourself
for pulling the trigger,
for finally, here comes my word.

You killed me,
and you killed yourself,
two dead bodies
wrapped as mummies.
I hope some century later
they discover this one
when love is gone!

The lost bones break down
the story of you, me,
and history of human beings.
The love and the lost,
the hate and the found,
make only one dead sound.

As the dust shakes off
from the brush,
these lyrics are the only piece of art,
the world in words,
our lives in letter of lies
and a tomb telling a myth of a heart.
What was a flood,
an open sea,
is a closed mouth
dressed in black.
It lights up the dark minded sky
in questions of who was I,

who was you?

There's this one
of many misspelled letters
next to the broken feathers,
bullets for lips,
and blood clips wings
crashing to the ground.

There is no sound.

Arrows

As much as I have
in my pocket
is this poetry armory strap;
It's his story time,
why don't you come over here
and sit on my lap?

I grew up as a late bloomer,
antonymous of a OK Sooner.
"Mario," all he is, is scraps.
Well why don't you come get a bone,
leave you
how your last leaves you.
One minus one
is you born alone.

You Found Me?
This isn't The Fray.
I come
and she may go like a stray.
I did it all backwards,
for she tried to collect her fall forwards
like a rocking chair.
The truth about this preservation
is something in a medium rare.

From learning a number,
to counting the times
she has left blame on a bed.
That sex over love
we called a cancer bow
injected with oxytocin;
Swimming in a pool of sun-kissed ocean
from fin to fin,
long enough to have burnt-out skin;
Turns a body into stitched nightfall veins,
and every typewriter artifact
leaves my archer's sutured trail.

Writing with medication
like a doctor,
living lies
like a truthful folklore teller.
Pleasure and non-stop drippin' pain,
what's the difference
when both sides feel
not enough of someone's everything?
Losing two dear ones is like zero
when subtracted,
and one goodbye *duece*
is forever remembered coming in twos.

Bang to pleasure,
bang to pain!
Fluttering words
are my arteries' coffin box,
beyond death in these secret arrows!

S.T.D. (Sexually Transmitted Demon)

At first it was no to my head,
then her body said yes,
like she was negative
when he still got it.
Was it the way you dressed,
or how you quickly it unzipped?
The bikini eyes,
or my stick you longed to drive,
and when it was in cruise control,
you couldn't stop feeding me.
I tried to tell you love wasn't organic,
built binging only on
any abandoned hormone.

You wanted to be wanted
from what was hard from me to hide.
I've given in to your thirst
unceasing it easy
starting in elementary,
and I have you lying and carving,
stealing those bones
at each bed cemetery.
I gave it to you,
passing it on through preserving lies,
the ones I transfer
in the mind as a scenic truth.
When I found
there was something missing in me,
I knew she was never mine.
She was surrendered as a share,
a devil's welcoming offspring offered at a dare.

I screwed her,
'cause she screwed me.
You always got out of it
what I put into it,
like everybody uses everybody,
transmitted love desperately.

So I'm continuing
the hammer at the rock,
detecting the look
at every mindful remain,
a STD.
Based on an Angel's tomb failing test,
it's my disease.
Like a virgin from what was wrong,
found you now loving
what you never liked to lose.
So every time she flips the switch of fake
or faithfulness for the day,
I hit the fuse for sparking fireworks,
those screaming lights
give her what she deserves.

It will never be over,
daily stitches a demon produced
trace her forever up at seducing skies.
By any means necessary,
eradicating the halo,
you asked to stay live,
like there really was no exit strategy,
once he's in,
he was never coming out.
Addiction was a friendly mind frame,
a picture perfect war
with recycled body parts
she gave everyone to find.
Who would have thought
a disease
could be what they badly needed?

A WOMAN'S DANCE

Only Through Your Eyes

I saw you dance,
went over
what your lips already said,
what he did,
and why I only saw myself
through your eyes.
Time after time,
your every blink
was more than goodbye,
more than silent night.

My fingertips revolving on
a zigzag space between lungs,
and your certified
surrendering smiles.
I knew this as a physic freedom.
Your heart that broke,
the one I could never bridge,
crushed every bit,
inch by inch.
I won't pretend
I can make it work,
I can't fix
and try to replace
a bitter feeling
with what I learned,
so we will let the maze of mistakes
find their burn.
No matter which invisible heartbeat
I want you to feel,
or wantin' you to walk
with new ambition high heels
some day you'll be in.
You must let faith drown
a reversible instinctive sin.
Please know I'm sorry
for everything he did.

Like the earth's water dance
around the shore
and the land's hold from the sea,
each night you lay,
your past and future waves of pain
die somewhere with me.
And I say one last time,
I only saw myself
through your eyes.
Your every blink
was more than goodbye,
more than silent night.

World's Dancing Detention

I go nowhere fast
deep into the ground,
leaving her
to dance across the floor,
with the pom-poms
arming someone else's cheers,
I collapse to the last part in tears.

At world's detention,
love proved to be
like hunger and thirst
constantly wanting
to feed yourself first.
Suddenly discovering
happily ever after
is only meant for a kid,
proving in love I walk
is my young forever daily myth.

A Reminder at My Feet

Standing alone in the dark
never seemed so hard,
so I creep into the morning;
Tying my shoes
and trying to forget
the old soles in me,
I learn how to slide
into the new life
I must survive in.
I sink by fury
when she can't say hi anymore,
and I'm force to flicker
the smile she once use to adore.

We chose to recite
our own philosophy,
leaving out that
the word of love
would implode like this.
Like a child's haunting boomerang,
the ring of your name
always brings back what I miss.
When the wind swirls
and thunder comes down,
I turn to the melody
that won't have me beat,
every sound keeps
a reminder at my feet,
wishing you walked along side me.

All Eyes on Miss Independent Lover

Ms. Independent Lover,
one day, one day
the entrance to your soul will blink,
asking, wanting
someone like me.
It doesn't matter now,
but it will when witnesses fall
one by one,
everyone who supplies you walks off.
Tired, lonely you ponder
burning a man's attempts
to show you love,
a window of opportunity
shuts before the rain comes in.
All you need is you?

The reminder is clear,
tear by tear,
Ms. Independent Lover,
locking your eyes on me
in the dark, begging
for some sort of spark.

I could kiss your soul
once more,
or remember?
It doesn't matter now
like before.

I fell into your house
by your seducing eyes
or were they both lies?

It was a trick
as parasites break down
walls of wood.

You come at me for forgiveness.

Now, I should?
But you would?

Every time the phone rang,
it was you calling convenience,
by the shock of your stare,
who is burning for grievance?
Insecure you lay in alarm
wishing to once again
claim my charm,
and you were content
to leave my scream
and escape all that was horrible.
Clockwise babe!
I too dealt with your bad hands.
Who is responsible?

Using me to find him
over and over
like a carousel.
What does wheel me here today?

When letters shatter
beautiful into ugly,
a tangent nature,
you will be holding onto
a shameful disordered honesty.

One day and one love
become two distances
never to be reached.
Ms. Independent Lover
all along I should have
avoided prolong, 'cause your eyes
were a beginning
to the end of the road.

I wish I knew, instead
I'm left with a thousand words,
Thousand miles to explain

a broken piece
in a irreplaceable heart.

Love is blind
and leaves you cold
finding a way to cope,
when you eye
some small lamp of hope.

Fallen and Frozen

As she precipitates,
this glass won't feel fool,
intoxicating a drug by storm,
yelling at his picture,
"Until there's no thought of you!"

Embellishment aside,
she wears it on her face
inside and outside,
something
the revealing cotton shape
can't hide.

You can see how
the drink is her weeping waste;
Eluding its truth as days pass,
liquids bring further decay,
it's easy to see
when the mirror begins to betray.

When you lose what she lost,
the world is unjust;
We acquire deceit
and turn resentment into a must.
Weather conditions
could never be clear,
running to disappear
inside that bottle,
all you will know is fear.

A club room snows in the blame,
for her heart is as frozen as a flake;
Oh freezing soul,
she thought she was in love,
how can she let
the rest of her life be a mistake.

The Heart You Face

Maybe I'm jealous
but baby I've seen this before,
there are wannabe's
designed in lies
so you'd remember
that dude's different names.
I wonder what you're doing
in and out of bars,
when a kiss of a boy
breaks your hopes in too many parts.

Like a dramatic movie,
clips here and pictures there,
that flirt you to a nightly disaster.
You could shake your head,
walk away then reach for the cell
and press send,
while I check the time,
foolishly stare down at the phone
waiting for a text or a call.
Somehow it will never ring;
You stay as close as a ghost.

Hunger for
the light up of your name
to read on the screen;
Instead the more I see,
the more every breath
rips this reoccurring dream
down seam by seam.

When I'm around you,
the more a heart breaks.
If I say the way I feel,
you might run;
If you agree,
we could fall in love,
or instantly say our goodbyes

and be done.
The faith as friends
turns to dust.

I want more,
this is all I'd forever fight for.
If I pursue, we could be wishing
we stayed how it was before.

I tell myself this is only me;
The fluorescence
in my patience is so bright
it has her blinded.
Babygirl whether Wayfare shades
on or off, they can't beat
the heart you face.

I wait and wait,
not cry or lie
to get one person
to feel this same kind of love
in return for me.
Dreaming for two of us to lock
the space between our lips,
forgetting there is a key.

She must know
any man should fall to their knees.

Give until it hurts;
Oh exhausting mind
she's all that I thirst!
Like roots in a rose for water,
who will weather
the growth of this limerence?

A soul asking for one chance,
living with the current
and the fantasy,
driving these veins inside of me.

Help!
God keep a secret at peace'
If I receive
a kind of undeserving rejection,
so long to pistons
in pursue-less passion.

Night Lie {John 3:20}

As she regularly pretends,
my mind don't mind,
I know the weak end
like everyone's photo feed
for a weekend.

She wants to come home
by the ring in the phone,
"Hello,"
I answer into the nightfall.
Always will be her,
I got "Lie" on the line.
He says,
"I'm no longer going to pursue,
you can't love another
if you don't love you."

Her body is the only potion;
The night is her pandering devotion.
He disappears
when she wakes up,
dancing in and out
devil's frame of mind;
As the star drops
and burns a soul,
the limelight she wants,
still a spark she can't find.
Cupid broke the arrow
long before the engagement,
death of intimacy as we know it.

Delusional
at what she looked for
or baby, is then
now loving her more!
The sun has vanished
from our bed sheets,
no more photo or synthesis;

No more you and me.
True love's portrait
never begins.

I was more attached to words
than with her.
Her clothes
never leave anything
up to a man's dream anymore;

Steps she erased,
love we made.

She's stuck
with trying to take back
every night before.

Rally for Life (A Missing Spirit)

She steps in front of the mirror
craving disaster,
beginning to lose trust,
obsessed with the face of fear,
she can't get a response
from any of us.

All too familiar
how people can be taken from you,
and people take you for granted.

It's time to fight on,
sometimes going in
has to be done alone.

That one day she finds
there's an untapped dream.
Forever or never collapses
at the world's stage,
wanting, waiting for you to move
in your next scene.
This is a rally for your life,
don't let others hate
your campaign, your drive.

When questions begin to sleep,
there is that one
we should always keep,
whether it will heal
or be all that we know is real,
live that dream baby.

Wear the pride,
deflect your insecurity,
their envy,
and wait for the heart's echo
behind the call of your name.
Your design is unrivaled,

the crowd will be sprung,
what you say
can't do them wrong!

She finds
she was singing this song
all this time;
To the ones next to her
and to the one
that can no longer be with her,
this message will display
across their mind.
Indefinitely, they caught
her cure of world divine.

Last One I Had

You were the last one to love.
I did go crazy,
a little bit more
dysfunctional than you.
When push comes to shove,
baby this is the truth,
I never sent you flowers,
that wasn't me.
So if any one tends to ask,
I'm doing fine, thanks.
I don't need you.
Only if they knew
what you caused,
only if they knew
what I lost.

You can say
what you need to say,
be with another man
to get you through the day.
We were a thunderbolt
that needed to break rain-free.

I'll hit you where it hurts,
you'll always hit me
where I deserve.
If I could look you in the eye,
I'd say, I don't need you.
I'm doing fine, thanks.
So if any one tends to ask,
I pleaded for forgiveness,
don't get it confused with you
being my only lifeline
for happiness.

This is my note,
a world currency.
I'll let everybody know, yes,

I'll take the king of all cowards,
for I never sent you flowers!
I know time will decide
the best I had,
as for now,
you're the last one I had.

Ex Girl

Did you hear
about him and her?
She broke his heart
like a Bastrop fire.
He's waking up to
what he has done,
pieces he sees
when he laces in the morning.
Pants won't fit the same,
and he begs to change
every association to his name.
She doesn't know
someone else plan
was for her to be my ex girl.

Dumb in love,
the game is this,
the only thing that last
is the first last kiss.
It's a short wick,
a new flame feeling
type of one moment affair.
She never knew
as I always did script;
Oh man, she should have thrown away
the match before a chance at forfeit.

This girl was like the last one,
who thought she won.

Shhhhh!
Look, I'm pregnant
in her thoughts
but she can't abort or deliver,
shame on me for loving her.

Maybe she had friends to lean on;
The one's spreading rumors like legs

that I can't find anyone new.
She doesn't know
two people's new lonely night,
as she dances
and figures a new way to twirl,
welcome to my ex world!

Did you hear
he only cared
about one moment in time?
The lock in their eyes,
skin tanned, and held between thighs.
My ex girl told a story,
like I'm the only one
that should have been sorry.

This is my lifelong affair,
not extramarital;
I never believed in one beauty queen,
I magnetically moved to any girl
that provided an idea
of a let me see that again scene.
Like Dalí, Michael Angelo,
and van Gogh,
who shouldn't have given me
the poetry painting light,
who conspires me to rip young hearts
and stay there sewing all-time low.
Repenting in torturing ink
where they don't belong,
for what every girl since her deserves,
welcome to my cowards!

Y.S.N.F (Young Sexy Nights Forever)

Let me tell you,
as we close our eyes
and release all tenderness,
I'm running out of breath
and you're dying to share,
am I a drug or hug away,
the line of symmetry is rare.

While this miracle
is one in the same,
love doesn't live in this frame,
so I'm going to break
the picture glass
and save face with hands.

Let me slide my fingertips
over the ocean current,
at the depth of the sands,
then lookup slowly
capturing the moonlight stars
one by one;
Our love made at morning sun.

Shame on this universe,
she stole the title.

Taken out of man,
God demands,
"Ask, it will be given,
seek and it will be found."
"I'll keep in touch,"
literally I reply
as sexual crackles become loud.
Let it flood until the end,
I stay content,
because her rain
never fails to eliminate my torment.

You tell me
when I feel your face,
have I touched your heart?

The hands of time axial
your body's core,
from head to toe,
lovin' you today
is always better
than a midnight's before!

Make Love Freely

Love with sex
is like a light for a cigarette,
this cancer you bring
is something I might regret.
Love with sex
is like a cloud
with the sounds of thunder;
This rain you bring
is something
I won't be able to weather.

I leave a chance
in a simile to make me
your love freely.

I pray you've seen inside
something more than a revolt,
a destine man to eternally hold.
Take the chance you need,
take the time you please;
A chance at forever
comes as quick as a second,
let the clock tick
into one lock of the lips.

Love with sex
is like a ride
with a fuel injection,
this fire you bring
is air to cause
a fatal suffocation.
Love with sex
is like a rhythm
with an endless beat;
This music you bring
is something I shouldn't
have stuck on repeat.

I leave a chance
in a simile to make me
your love freely.

You're a desired infection,
undoubtedly, your skin paints
an undying mental impression.
Into the night, we have contact,
an epidemic attraction
at your eyes,
a distance city
where I long to reside.

To make love freely
is what we have in common,
curing our division
with her stimulation;
It could never be made clearer,
her goddess physique
brings us nearer.

Heaven Began, Love Again

You see,
you've been riding in
and out of my mind
all this time,
like a cyclist,
spinning and contesting
if I could love again,
asking in my dream
when you're near,
am I beat
by the race of my heart?
Afraid to lose once more,
baby, you know it's you I adore.
Ready to entrust,
starting and finishing
the rest of my days with you.
I want to show
how heaven began,
only, when I love again.

In the life after,
these tears the past left us
evolve into wings,
where you've been
and where I should be
will fly you to me.
We've landed in no secret,
our lips will lock forever away.
I swear I'll show
how heaven began,
God knows,
he's assembled this soul
for only you to conceal,
a crush into something real,
no longer
a heartbreaker's sexual steal.

Go Around

It's weird how music
can take you to a place,
as the track goes on,
you replay shared times.
Those days never fail to ask
how did I end up here?

All things considered,
I stayed away
from making new friends;
My luck had enough,
not done out from fear,
because I only wanted you here.

Years pass, I was tired
of singing in circles,
the love song go around
doesn't seem so merry,
dizzy falling
and unconsciously melting
everything bit of lonely.
Replayed dedications,
that damn radio kept you alive,
thinking what would you say
if we danced
all the way
onto your door step?

Would you understand?

Same ole picture
or would you see
a new man?
Would tears rush down
from our eyes,
like the avalanche
in a winter cold
that won't go away?

There is a list
when I wish
I had one last talk,
how regret sunk
when I watched you walk.

Love isn't lies,
sometimes it needs
two unselfish tries.
It's the wrap of two hands
around a soul,
a touch of lips
eclipsing enough light
in a bloody night.
I never took it in to let us grow;
Time is young.
Oh baby, let me speak
how many ways I was wrong!

I'm here,
I'm hanging by a glimpse
as I see you turn,
stopping, leaning into me;
The world can never win,
whichever way it will spin.
We lose ourselves in jealousy,
but then it hits me,
you're the only one kissing me,
not out of fear;
You only want me here.

Beside the fights
and emotional highs,
I am me
because of losing
and recapturing you,
like regardless of the time,
those moments you gave in,
love came back around
from the downward spin.

Butterfly Blessings

What a blessing,
the way you look at me,
fireflame dreams
meet reality
above the coldest peak,
project no limit in eternity.
Oh *mi corazon*,
my never have to be alone!

Our feet step in
snow of a mountain range;
The butterflies of you,
cause seasons begging to change.
When you're away
the monarch
keeps your flight alive;
Ruler of my heart,
ruler who aligns the stars
when I can't see;
The queen
who illuminates our world;
We suddenly believe.

I walk,
it lands down in me,
rushing stronger than gravity.
Palms sweat in
and out the fever,
this feeling can't last forever;
No need for thermostat,
smile after smile
how could it stay on track?

What a blessing
to bring all I need,
the sun to capture winter,
shivers in and out
one night fever;

Oh this feeling has to last forever?

Maybe it started
with metamorphosis,
and a persistent patience
to I promise you this,
the cycle will be reminded
when we make that first kiss.

Rocking Chair

He texted her,
"I don't want you anymore!"
Always back and forth,
game of tag,
but we never had it.

I can't be addicted
to the phone anymore;
It's an hourglass
for every girl
that doesn't last.
They turned love
into a rocking chair,
back to the future
tech-chain reaction;
Always moving on
and never intimately consuming.

She shackled every dream
to the floor,
while he built her grave
like here comes
the handy tool man,
ready with the wrench
twisting our own
stupid cupid thoughts.

She never stopped asking,
"Did something happen to you,
to have you with voices
as screws being so loose?"
I said,
"Tighten yours up,
do you ever close your mouth?"

I pulled the chair
and her memory still fell.
We went back to the hit

of that same seat,
all people ever did
was use their knees as feet.
There's no such thing
as a king here to bow for,
and princesses don't exist;
Fairytales are rocking chairs
which swing and miss,
like her calls were guiding books,
the happily ever after ring script
we madly ignored.

Faith and Time as One

Why can't I find a soul like hers?
Truthful in discipline,
my friend before we seek;
It's time to be united within.
She left with my faith
on her wrist,
where did time go?

Maybe I can't stay away
from a domineer girl,
phonetic drugs
and control as their hope,
their lonely way to cope.

Man of faith,
believing love
rather be injected
and it isn't a criminal myth.

We are together
when she said,
"I feel so alone."
Speaking rhythms of wisdom,
hungry to be loved,

aren't we all?

Love Chamber, You Never

I chase after you
with my words,
obviously, my actions
can never give a woman
what she deserves.
Maybe I'm not aggressive;
Surely I'm connective,
like the tissue in my heart;
My lipids are tempted
to feel abandon weight of this love?

When dictated by those eyes,
kidnapped by one glimpse,
you never could
grant a man one wish
for one touch of the lips.

Love can be
so damn simple,
but you locked it in a chamber
like a vicious ventricle,
so there goes an indictment
in a cynical cycle!

Who will hold your fear?
Bring a tissue for your tear?

There goes my heartbeat
racing to you,
never going to tell you
I told you so,
I'll listen,
and let my silence show,
your crazy insecurity;
The need for attention
in a witness.

You forget truth

like a bad case of dementia;
When the judge dismisses,
you wish you did have dementia,
because blank page pain follows
like once upon a time
when my written heart did.

Haunted and never misguided,
I always did supply it'
Running through my veins,
visible with my words,
you never let my actions
lead you to believe
it was what you deserve!

The love chamber
caused the linger
of losing your mind
for unnoticed
now noticed crime.
What have we committed?
They say it always takes two,
fool me none,
shame on you!

Lone Star Ice (Fallen and Frozen Part II)

There goes my hesitation
for a hand on another glass routine;
Apnea carousel for a home
in wake me up baby,
feel the blow.

Weighted on my stomach,
crushin' out of bounds,
notification ring
proud of the next man
repelling in you;
The pounding gut whistle
started in bed
and consciousness anew.

I told her not to sin in Texas,
she continued to text me about us.
She couldn't choose a man,
so every love had did a chance.

Her size of a lone state kissed me,
like I clipped my skin with every shave.
Phone therapy told to keep hittin',
no glove to mix Aurora's pudding.

Hands laid dirty,
bury me!

Bury me,
conspire an enemy affair
to sea like Bin Laden.
The thing about a slave is
we are born from a world trade;
From those chains
gave us a game,
frontcourt and back of the sail
composed undue women;

Dimes and her half-way there types,
brunette or blondes,
Jackie and Marilyn;

Here, my rumor mill
Catholic confession.
Like the times of JFK,
she danced her confusion
to be an iconic flake,
leaving anchor shaped hearts
stuck in the frozen snow.

The darker the drink got,
the more revolts she taught;
New wine sleet
to rock hard whiskey ice,
fresh age Monica Lewinski
peaches in a lie.

Happiness EXist

It felt like days removed,
she saw him
with the girl she use to be.
Not one more drink too soon;
Unborn to the new game,
she could never understand the ink
when it doesn't match the same pen.

Long and faded hair
on the floor across from tears
and chills damp
in an unwrapped pillow sheet,
Tramadol winds
and alcohol fires kept us safe.
She said I wanna fuck
'til you find open
our new basement
for a heart break grave.

Dead nine times
from a familiar
friend cloud above;
When life is never
done heavenly,
no one knows what it is,
even as their dry whispers persist;
Happiness exist
when lies come alive
on a lonely night.

You're killing him
with tiny kisses,
another pause in the moan,
and those flashes
of the one she truly misses.
No choice
but for her to exploit
the pain in pleasure;

The bed constantly feels as fine;
She'll rule and decide
when one shall die.

Immortal commas
play the party on and on,
like Billie Jean's lyricon.
She like a beauty queen,
crowned and crucified
to that same ole smile in disguise.

A Man This Mad

She came to be exhausted
from that everyday guy she got.

If she loves him,
what did she do with her kiss?

Is that always the same kind of girl
I could never dismiss?

I fell,
still fallin' into her,;
Hearts done
gone mad,
animosity,
straight up;
She never gave me
my own velocity;
We moved at her stand still,
arms up, lips tied down,
and body too magnetic to be
boyfriend detach.

I guess in
became too detailed,
all this time
she had been jailed?
Who had the key?
I said
she needed her individuality
from a routine mind's infidelity;
Absent of especially,
what she already had,
I swear
she never
touched a man this mad!

Tape

There's yellow tape
to the entrance of her heart.

They say
one coward of man
should never follow another,
but somehow
a woman's weakness is
two other people's strength.

He fell asleep
next to that tape,
waited outside for a cure
inside a rebound
of her unrecognized self-hate;

I am the one
ready here
to cleave
cold blame
at the gate.

Playground Days (Revelry Child)

There came in
out of the fishin' line
what rarely crossed her mind;
For our remembrance,
we all give up space for lent,
50 days after the 40,
benefits in penance
should always kick in.

Right now
from all that's built in a past,
she made you feel
like you won every first place.
A trapped exhibit
of one forever scene;
I'd say,
she use to be a picture perfect
in a shopping window screen,
attached to every
beautiful edge of a border.

Her soft skin
talkin' that talk,
pages and sheets all the same,
oh she began to use him
like a pillow case.

Rain's kiss as my passenger,
drizzle drivin' sounds
became pouring words
for how nothing ever grown,
a lightning root
felt impact on my skin
like two towers being blown.

Earthquake and hurricane
designed birth days;
Your world born in mine,

visiting hours are over,
what does it matter?

Dreams never broke hearts
but built bridges
when reality did enough damage.

Trust only cracked smiles
and faithful pills that flew her
from cliff to cliff,
like stolen refugee clouds
for everyone to come out
of the evergreen lift.

She said my veins
ignited playground days.
I'm sorry,
I'm later than growing
and crushing on you sooner.

Give me your eyes
as they dare not cut deeper than
what I had before,
because I've been hurting,
patient, waiting for her
to see an image
of what God made in her.

One look from her to him,
a quarter century metal
has been turned to dust,
next to one sculpting rock
in a lost of their young
live foolish lies.

Others had one day
too many
to inspire,
while he had one hour
and lips threw him

into her floors of fire.
Media friend of flames
crumpling a download sky stream,
the world watched his atriums
ripple at revelry city's seam.

Finally Speak

Baby, if I knew you would leave,
and if you never gave a chance
to say goodbye, and
if you spent all your days
with the ones you love,
without me to see you grow,
to see you bloom;
Knowing you found more
than the roots in truth,
I'd be happy, I'd be glad.

If you had another ring
around your finger,
while my mind forces
a face to linger,
I'd be happy, I'd be glad.

If you lived to dance,
and if I had to watch
a different lead,
to see my shadow removed
and you found
all the bliss
that came to you,
I'd be happy, I'd be glad.

For there is a light
that today glows
in my mistakes that burned
and made his turned as vows.

If you forget
the memory
behind my name,
and how the cuts
proved to fill your change,
I'd be happy, I'd be glad.

You'll see,
you'll get to meet
the new me,
as long as I stay on this track
in having one thing,
in something to believe;
I'll be inside a heaven,
where we can finally speak.

Daddy's Scars and Family

Hotel Home

She didn't say much,
tired of shouting lakes for eyes,
she closed the door,
that always said enough.
Some type of demon felt inside,
a hotel as a home
was all they traveled for,
the new starts in checking out.
She was the one going on
stuck on love,
while he stared at clocks
until they painted a picture,
like the hands of time
always reminding him
of when they did move.

Reality had no worth
in being real,
the idle cracks dared space to see
what it would steal.
Was she running out of games?
Was he running out of mistakes?

He wasn't familiar
with the smell in the sheets,
and she woke up crying,
wishing her dreams
had never came true.
Sleeping with another
but falling into you to see
how long it would last,
it wasn't cheating
if it meant someone else is believing.
Her father taught
that hits were okay to take,
and mom knew
the lies in a true drunk,
together stuck them on love.

The house was screaming
for a way out,
the pieces fit but bricks
were quickly crumbling down.
No matter the thickness
in the blood,
it was the damage
her bed-night dancing took,
like an addiction
from an intimate drug.
The more the band played,
the more bottle caps
and flames piled on;
Some how the suitcase stayed,
wheels still swirled
toward any broken home
that came along.

Daddy's Scars All Alone

Wondering how did I
capture the film rights to
a generational military news clip book
rebuilding his face?

Mom said I grew up on base,
like in and out a mobile home;
not some Hollywood movie trailer.
Father had no choice
but to protect his financial securities,
while he left the children
with his wife all alone.

This is the blue and red dream,
strap breadwinner with a gun,
helicopter army man,
and training missions,
until a politicians' manifest destiny
is on a non-stop finish.

We began to know the man above
when daddy's Chinook crashed;
Ambulance colored scars
turned into the only stories,
PTSD, and a family
forever left in worries.

He couldn't walk,
so mom had to
hand the kids to grandma.
He screamed
with being screwed
in every jointing bone;
She fought, took a hit,
But determined not to
let him feel all alone.

It sucked at his blood,

but this was no fictional fairytale
like Twilight;
This is the real thing.
Grandma couldn't take
one more death;
Saw one die in Vietnam,
so it was a rosary spirit
she hand spoon-fed.
From a new Mexican dream,
America lost more self-esteem;
Suing and deaths came one by one,
forcing builds around
a child educational fund,
and how we didn't know war silent the fun.

When mom said
reach for the stars,
their sons could only
begin to wonder
living inside daddy's scars.

Trade Songs Like Tears

Tell me who is born happy?
Smiling before
any kind of pain is felt,
spineless like a blueprint skyscraper
before its stories are built.

Mom gave me
this tune of a mouth
to bring the world;
Something it never wants to see,
my tears, the next best voice to believe.
I'd trade death to have life,
I'd trade my secret to end this fight.

My brother, father,
and his father chased bars;
I guess I did too but I never lied.
I had to survive where they didn't,
and finish what they couldn't.

Maybe it was
the touch of a dishonest girl
that kept my mother bleeding.
Black trash bags thrown
from place to place,
I still carry mom's cries
running down hers and my face.

I'd trade this song to undo
those who did a child wrong.
Maybe that's why I ran away
when college time was up;
I had to grow
into something positive,
to find someone to teach me
how to live
outside someone else's scars.

Writing through distance and time,
my only musical puncturing beat,
scratching for another tomorrow,
like a disease patient praying
for a delivery in new bone marrow.

He Walks Unknown (Father Where Are You?)

We're all someone unknown,
it may seem like a contradiction,
but you can't see stories
like the calcium that feeds your bone.

To those who will never be,
that chose to put volunteer forces on blast,
he'll be the fastest substance to be absorb,
like Usain Bolt, it's no Jamaican joke.
Yah *mon*, that absurd!

He'll tend to stomach and excrete,
anything that un-breaks you
from your knee.
He's tired of impatience;
You don't move
but you certainly
run your mouth.

It's time
to chew on bookworms;
Don't be afraid,
he'll digest you instantly.
Once he's done with you,
you're going to have to
swallow this protein.

Yup, bring the milk
from the cow,
graze, he said graze
a heart's land;
This is home,
must you ask how?

He'll bring the lead
like pen that ignites a revolution;
This is an AED.
Your solution

for you to finally cleanse an evil,
from our similar recovery.

You still can't see his movement,
one on each side of the nose,
two electric shocks
when a face making a pose.

Oh you have to stop and stare,
put on your shades to protect its glare.

Daddy use to say,
"Let's get drunk
and be somebody."
Euphorically, he will always be there,
and he didn't have to take a sip.
You must know this power,
light it up more than
a 13-day nuclear shower!

The world is done over;
He came, he saw,
before you knew what hit.
He doesn't ever miss like Albert Pujols.
He is the unknown distance
between the release of a pitch
and the cork of a bat;
Too funny,
there goes the crack of your laugh.

You better believe,
he shouldn't have to be
crucified again
out of your citizen pleasure.

Face of Place(s)

You are everything
that begins with beautiful.
For all those
worry free wrinkles,
they happen
to happen over time.
Face of life,
of a world,
not of useless age;
It is my lasting impact,
the matter of true arts' loving fact.
Mona Lisa,
she can hasta la vista.
No proof needed
for a picture,
you're a living story.
Glance this way,
stand still
and look at me,
I'll tell you the tale:

You froze my fears,
and you dried my tears.
When you feel
like your face is running,
and you're far from stunning,
think the opposite,
think of this;
It's 'cause you were too busy,
tender with us boys,
rightfully too uneasy.
Making a place,
giving a catering taste,
for this one, and that son.
Like the sun,
giving light to the can't be done,
you gave life, the ignited faith.

When no one asked,
when no one told,
you built my soul.
You repaired it at times,
through your eyes,
when you knew
I could no longer live from lies.

So when you look,
it's the mirror in my views
that say you're everything
that begins with beautiful.
You show how love works,
and how it will compose,
with one look on your face,
I see every single place,
where I've been,
where I'm going
and where I'm from.
Thank you mom.

The Hands Memory Left Clocks Dying
(In memory of Aurora Adame and Sulema Martinez)

My blood was rushing today
in one place,
until I woke up
it had spilled across the floor.
Finally, finally,
I'm ironing out for a new face.

Head snapped
for this is no dream?

My tear fluid ran away,
away like an endless stream,
rained down
by her fifty, fifty chance.
On everyone's count
asystole read zero,
between crying and denying,
no faith, no umbrella
for a hero.

I had a tissue
in one hand,
and the other
couldn't believe
the flex of misuse,
cleaved to leave
the land of heartless.
Heartbreak had been
ripped and ripped;
Praying it can be sewn,
I laid here alone.

Looking at them,
he gets to take her
and vice versa,
over and over again.

Where is my heaven?

Tell me, tell me!
Let it ring now!
How I am dying,
really dying somehow?

What good are hands
if they can't hold,
can't touch,
can't feel.

Time will dismantle
the current once more,
while oceans watch the clock
in a jammed anchor reel.
Yeah people come and go,
but if you knew
what I know,
you'd have a picture
with no memories to show,
and those eyes
wouldn't remember my name.

We lost too many years of a life
dedicated to helping me see,
what's not there
and what I felt
turned a child to believe.

While she let me live
in this life sentence,
a premeditated path;
I was already put to death,
because purposely
no one was going to be left.

God was like a ghost
living when you don't need him
and disappearing when you do,
it's like the sympathy
for a rosary shadow,

which we dare not
feel or hold,
only view.

No skin can win what kept
your unconscious touch so real.

I hate you God,
I hate you too;
Look what we have in common,
oh the thought,
a delusional body of symptoms;
The mind learned
absence from love;
I can see why we fought.

Closing Wound

Look at me
and join the flood;
Splashing red sea,
this open wound is coming,
finally pouring down;
Here I come,
the puncture is done.
See you soon.

Take it, evil has lived
floating in my hormones.
The wave, please,
I beg for postpones!

It's numbing
starting at the brain, leaking
from the only one that excretes,
nothing left anymore
beating these nerves so discrete.
Bleed! Bled through every moment;
Oh I forget how it happens?

The bolts and screws
can no longer be covered
or fasten;
Oh exposure, oh now,
I get some sort of closure?

This open wound,
you can hear my soul sound;
I'll see you soon.

Piano plays
key-by-key,
good to an unwanted bye.
The choir voice
admits an amazing mistake,
our human mistake.

Let me have my grace
with tragic infections
as needles revamped these bones,
decaying from how
you left me astray.

This is saving grace
with an open wound,
I'm done bending at the altar;
I always liked sooner than later.

I'm dying,
dying to live again;
Let me die
oh please!
God let us die,
this open wound
has to take it this last time.

Whispers of Roses
(In memory of Aurora Adame)

I still hear whispers of roses,
one by one,
as wreaths peel off.

Playground days
along footsteps of an open heart,
where trails disappear
but we swear it had been there.

Tell me are you here?

Wrinkles must turn backward,
please force me back
into yesterday,
bring her here today!

Child Don't Cry

She finished school
without knowing a friend.
Didn't walk the stage,
but walked a thin line;
Some boy knocked
and ran before any door
began to open.

Four letters changed
the road of what could have been,
b-a-b-y,
three months short of a year,
brought for
the rest of my life struggles
about true fear.

No men, no father,
a lonely bird
figuring its new feather.
Teenage dream,
turned into
a couldn't sleep scream;
All that came out was,
"Child, don't cry
mommy's here.
Day and night
I make an oath,
it will always be us both.
Daddy has a new girl,
so he can't be with
you and I."

It's a shame,
I sometimes see him running
when I look at my baby in the eye.

Heartless fairytale
turned into one more.

She told herself
no breaking down,
my baby is growing up.

Sad songs
couldn't make her feel
the real thing;
No man was gonna kiss
her baby goodnight.

The child got use to goodbyes,
different cribs,
and when she cried
in the lonely dark,
she always knew mommy's lips.

All that came out was,
"Child, don't cry
mommy's here.
Day and night
I make an oath,
it will always be us both.
I can't blame the rain,
it gave me you, baby.
Let me feel the storm;
Baby, I found love
when you were born."

A Dawning Love, San Antonio to Austin

I sit at the table
with father always in the right,
and mom's loving armed my side.

When you have one life,
what I will miss is this:
New found days
down at the lake
where there's only a thought of peace;
Running in and out of our hometown,
where my soul can never leave.
Staring eyes upon the burnt lit tower,
where dreams they said,
"It is yours to capture!"

When it all flashes by,
said and done,
I pray they will remember
this one from their baby son.

We will always struggle to find
what we can do,
and if today was my last day,
it doesn't go wasted
to now think things thru.
Having another chance
to learn how to act;
Remove the greed, say, "Yes,"
and take all the "I can't" back!

Son, "The TV needs to be shut off,"
too many hours we watch,
"Child, you should be
outside showing this world
your type of love."

I let divine reactions spin,
week by week;

They ask what is
the stimulation I seek?
In return I say,
"Maybe it was
a family's hidden disease
that made it real.
Maybe it was God's voice
in a last cardiac rhythm.
Caskets that we saw cry,
making church mass
have a numb feel."

There always lad a lesson
from the dying
and a reason for forgiving;
It starts at the table,
dressed in a dawning love,
for each breath
a guide for a new way,
knowing recreation
can start today.

A Tribute From This Root

As this Silent Sunrise story unfolds,
going down Elrod and Connally
on the same road,
a branch of the same tree,
where can I be?

Must be home,
a selfish kind of love
that will never disconnect,
full of my mirror's reflect.
In 360 degree
unbearable rapid motions,
there's never a surprise;
A Dove Flight speeds up faith,
when I have nothing left,
when I'm tired of running and hiding;
At the table our Sister's prayers
keep us fighting.

It comes from the oaks,
this ageless branch.
The cries, a brother's battle,
the names
and their laugh unconditional,
a Catholic kept traditional.
A constitutional idea
that can't die
as long as we place action
on the dream in our words.
We weren't going to be the Kennedy's;
Ask not,
but we keep their same remedy.

The lock that never changes its key;
In one twist of the knob,
there's a bark of the millennium dog,
and the door that opens faith's true love.

Five houses down,
now there's a frown
as he turns it up.

It comes from the oaks,
leafs that will continue to grow
young as long as forever goes.

When you come here
you will see,
down Irma Avenue,
the fame composing *Tejano* records;
Near Edgewood,
a discipline of military men
and the touch of a grandmother's hand.
The '69 Cambodia fight
that took his young life,
the two burn crashes
that took daddy's newspaper heart;
The cancer smoke
that keeps us guilty missing.
From a first dance
under a neon moon
and Mel driving me out of hell,
we learn to revitalize
souls and backbones.

No storm can raid my house,
no casket can end this
in our life's time;
From one blood to another,
this root continues to run.

When there's any doubt,
my passage can help remind,
this is Texas;
However long it takes us
to branch this six flag state,
eyed on the new American dream,
where an Alamo style

courageous Warren Warrior
resides in me.

The oaks will get you hooked
up I-35 and my favorites
will take you for a ride.
How legendary
50 feels 21 in our Spurs;
I remember, it was the game,
which coordinated
our passionate community cohesion.
Misty through the oaks,
this is where
an eternal family tree grows.

Some Sad Song

I had it at its worst
and at its best,
everything in between;
I know sometimes
it all feels the same.

Running from anyone
that can stop a bleed,
time and time again,
listening to a friend can be a cure.
Save, seal, and deliver
this word of mouth
that in silence you can read.

Don't speak,
I see the sutured jaw,
and when you
begin to touch and trust,
there is a phonetic pause
still surrounded by a broken law.

Baby, welcome to this world;
Welcome to my world.

We pump a fist,
trying to curl
the diamonds
and a pearl.
But gold only lies
in an internal core,
something eyes tend to ignore.

Is there a reason
your heart shuts
like your eyes
when you pray?
Ask and ask God

for a reason for you to stay?

Evil is taken out of devil,
'd' drops in death
and in the vitamin
that drives your lifeless skin,
like a baby removed
from the one who chooses abort,
and a tomb of fear
left as a natural resort.

When we erase a life
using Plan B,
like effortless error of a pencil,
it's easy to understand
the world's violence
a future child will see.

There always is some sad song
reminding you of a mistake.
Trying to forget and fake
it never happen;
So, we pop pills
to keep eyes blind,
like the hallucination of Ambien.
Sweet dreams always
make us remember reality,
sleeping to the best
and living in the worst.
Constant trips into heaven
and out of hell,
afraid to relive memories
that map the times we did fail.
Migrating in grace,
and at clip of the night's airfoil,
we're back to square one
like the roots in the soil.

So you drink up
to get your BAC up,

euphoria and ethanol
in the bloodstream,
with a hint of nicotine,
known to kill
but we refill constantly.
Reality becomes guilty,
once facing bars behind DWI.

Couldn't control your vehicle,
slamming the brakes
into a parent's child.
If that was your offspring,
you wish you could undo the tread,
wishing to press rewind
on this song
to remind you of a basic wrong.
Turn back time,
turn the wheel on a stolen life,
for a baby will never see elementary;
A mother and father
lowering that 2 by 2 casket
at the cemetery.

I suppose we are daily
digging our grave;
Similar to trying to find gold
in the beginning of this tune;
Ignoring any religious feature
and friend that can generate a save.

Receipt

Saw my life past by me today,
I couldn't believe this feeling
would ever be possible;
I didn't think to shop,
I had to let love pop this bubble,
grab life by the handle
in an empty bottle.

They say, I'm easily influenced
by my general vicinity;
Whether eyeing hell
or smiling at the heavenly,
I try to fill my glass up with multiplicity.
We have to taste this
to know that
shouldn't go to waste.

By a crave in one love desires,
I found some friendly hearts
are grown into respect;
in a collapsing city
or a isolated town.
Others who ran away,
and those who fought the wave
before they could drown.

We'll mind their space
and let them be alone,
then answer the call
when it's time to roll;
Eventually, we hit the bar
when lights go low,
for booze sometimes
let's our true spirit show.

Friends naturally become
like receipts,
a reminder

where we come and go;
Put value in life's transactions,
maybe placed as God's witnesses;
Kept in our pocket full of faith
to never be thrown away or escape.
It's okay to pile up receipts
that turn into drinks;
As long as our goal is to capture
our self as a whole.

There will always be that girl
at an inconvenience wasn't the right fit;
By an unthinkable emotion
that had my fellas wishing for a return,
however, there was something to learn.

To my homegirls,
there will always be that one guy
who you didn't know
could be one special;
By ignorance has you crying
for exchange and some sort of refund.
To both sexes,
I know it's hard to believe,
the one you are meant to love
has already come.

Let's pick up receipts
where they leave us;
Places kept by footprints
in any hardship,
certifying friendship.

God's will is to always send a friend
in helping us suspend.
Begin to take interest in a stranger,
when times become a lil' stranger.
He and she can be the one you need;
Differentiating love from lust,
they can buy the wine that unwinds

fermentation to the make of trust.
Preach what is available
and the never going to be suitable,
sanity for a time he felt weak,
and humbling hours at work
she counted down during the week.

Add a true friend in your diet
and tag these words,
because when hate
provides too much debt,
friends can give all the world's credit back.
An eternal gift registry
defined by a lifetime warranty.

Tickin' Tears

Today, a thought had life,
I brought you back to mine.
When you picked up
everything I dropped,
how when you left the bed,
it laid so soft.
You listened with silence,
my lil' soothing presence.

I struggle,
how can I put you to sleep?

In the beginning,
you use to cry with every clock's tick,
now, every memory fits
the reason for my shoe's lace;
A string and its tie on your bone,
but who will be there to touch
when I feel alone?
Who's going to be my only fan
when I come home?

A decade passed by,
I can think of how
you brought years to my life.
It's your inches that help me grow,
to be at peace,
to empty fear at what I now know.

Are you at the door?
Say yes?
Your eyes always said it best;
Those invisible tears,
the one's you save
coming down mine.
All I can feel,
all want to see
is you there

when we're at our final rest.

Heartbreak comes
with the missing,
'cause it's the spirit
that has us fishing.
It's left with you,
those places we go
in search for hollow happiness,
those many times
you were my only shadow;
Today, I look outside
I can't find you through the window.

Is there a heaven for you,
I hope,
you were more than this thought,
my companion to help one cope.

What You Face

These days the bed lays cold,
disguised as a three times over
Russian roulette type of sleep;
Wondering when I wake up,
how he made it
through the ambulance alarm?

Most days people catch me
in a photo lit stare;
Why you so mad?

"No, motivated."
I'm thinking
about paralyzing fire
my dad lived through;
from the helicopter crash,
to losing his brother in Vietnam.
His father died in his teens;
A 28 year-old with two kids
learned to walk again,
destine by his wife
to make his family ends.

How no one ever knew
the one of a kind man?

No more pain,
for happiness sake
let me take the tears;
God not yet,
don't you dare clock a ticket.
You and mom are my faith.
When the pretty young things
do me wrong,
and I'm struggling to find my place;
Young forever,
I look to the mirror,
smile,

recognize my problems
are nothing
compared to
what you face.

HOW WE LIVE: A WORLD'S WAR

How We Live

The moments we live
depleted and people
still ask to give;
Endless bargains
that turn into bribes,
and favors convert
to a spine full of knives.

A cruel road that causes drift,
when waiting produces no tip.
I could get thin or pretend,
live off lies of saturation,
have sex, inject drugs
as chief stimulation;
Watch purpose
turn into poison,
or promote fear
to gain coition.
Call it sexist,
call it pessimistic,
or an approach of Evelyn's mystic.
Play God with dice,
deduce until wrong feels right.

Is it in you,
is it in I,
what does the future possess,
a world where
a dream is considered protest?

Our Only One Moment

It's not Mayday,
when a signal threatens
the fall of our day,
it's a dare to crash into love,
racing as one.
These pieces we feel,
fill our way,
breaking a life
into years of one moment in time.

Tomorrow never guaranteed;
It will only take a second
to set you free.
Another chance
at last to eject relapse;
Do you dream
of taking words back?

Fossilizing stories
from our decaying facts,
uncovering all along
we loved motionless,
leaving clocks to rotate
a reserved hand on afraid,
while truth rested another on unsaid.

Why pick up the phone?
Did you say hi
because you knew
they were blinded anyway?

Or did goodbye,
steer you here alone today?

A hopeless before
is once upon a time;
Tomorrow can no longer be rerun.

Praying on flickers
to lead the lost;
This is our only one,
a light channeling the darkness,
along sounds of feet
stepping into forgiveness;
Any time when
the past shouldn't last
and a moment is held tight;
These arms become,
will always be
an extension of my heart,
with a hug,
saving sane is where we start.

Thoughtful Moments

This is what matters the most,
flakes and snakes,
sinners or saints;
Life may hate
but carry restraints.

This is what matters the most,
lock your faith
dispose the key;
Could be,
can always see,
resides in we.

This is what matters the most,
when you find your soul,
block out the world
and the words you're told.

This is what matters the most,
waking up to where you want to be,
it's not far,
oh so close to amended tendency.

The Voice Continues on Broken Records

They ask why
I'm so nice to the ruthless?
Maybe 'cause they will never
get those things they miss.

You don't know what love is,
let go of the lone faith,
poet-hero!
Trying to change
the game of life
like the Bambino,
but Ruth struck out more times
than he connected;
He's still the greatest,
with the fame.
The orphan never rejected.

I try to do it
for the better,
so their mistakes
won't batter up
the world I live in.

Guinea pigs shouldn't become
chemical weapons to destroy us,
like IS shouldn't ever be WAS,
like once upon a time
when the world was one.
I'll let the losses
be the reason why I won;

Like a delicious steak,
I'm havin' that;
I'll take the fork out the road
and remove a knife from my back,
eat with the steroids
and what you've grown,
then take the high road.

I could go on swinging
the barrel of my bat
and unload, or turn the metal
into something more gentle,
like a stone from my heart.
So you can build
your own house with it
and stop blowing mine down,
like the wolf did it to the three.

Build your company,
the vaccine,
without me
or please fabricate
a bridge in between.
You can think twice
before you cross
or figure out
I'm cut from a different cloth.

Double me and create two,
I'll run with the real thing in me
and you can keep the clone;
Let it be sounds
of the broken record,
the reason why you're alone.

I can't save the young
or be the only one strong,
whether I give a lung,
the voice will continue on.

Do you! Let her be
that not to do.

Here comes
less of a friend,
the sign with the Dead End,
'cause if I throw you a lifesaver

while your cries
flood your own levee,
you'll get confused how to hold on;
By swing with the guard,
you would still choose to drown.

How sad,
what makes you think
this is the reason why I'm mad?

I know we lose
or try to steal off
someone else home plate
like a suicide squeeze,
cheat on your love,
your main squeeze.
But the minute we get caught,
we say please!

It's always hit and run,
do what we have to do
to be legendary,
like the batter in this homerun king,
or invent a new defensive mechanism
like Tom Landry.

See this literary art attack
as the king of wishful thinking,
back, back, back, gone,
pass the warning track,
so long, I'll keep this theme song.
When two lungs squeeze out the center part,
you can move on,
in your own movie,
choose a new beginning
and a possible alternate ending.

P.S you can turn back to mine,
anywhere in the video book
you can always rewind,

and unburied deep will be
a beating heart you find.

My soul will be wrapped
in a open casket
with regrettable living concepts,
for all they were
is a pinch nerve to test,
in flexion, relaxation, or termination,
some we passed
and most we looked past.

What Did I Miss

Tell me what I missed?

Don't want me to speak;
You say silence is the best.
Unsaid is understood,
what's the use,
what am I to do?
I'll be fine by you?

The heat never felt so cool,
after water spills down
from the sun skies,
from the fight in between our eyes.
You say there aren't any boundaries,
no ground to be had;
I'll take my so called angry
and your glad, move the sand
from an ocean,
leave your love,
your flood.

Say nothing at all,
and release your potion,
like the sun
hitting each one of us with its rays.
Yes, I guess I'm the only one
who misbehaves!

Why did I ever leave?
Maybe it is knowing
I could come back at anytime,
mastering clocks to
automatically rewind,
and possessing something better
recorded in mind.

I never did stress,
simply progress,

into another period,
like I'm trying to get out of English class.

Life is written too fast,
never getting a chance to
reread a script,
I jump to the next pad,
like a frog trying to metamorph
into something new;
hop on the train before it hits the track.
One-way trip
'cause I'm never coming back.

What stays,
never happen here?
We want to forget out of fear;
Purposely, history explodes
in your face.
Exhaustively, it takes place
once more,
every time you enter
the same blowback door.

Once you listen to your heart,
the mirror says
something different,
what you become
is what people
know your silence isn't.

Back words

You will spin my words,
and assume more cowards.
I say, you say,
and you believe I deceive.

As space irritates love dissipates.

Claim to refrain so tears retain.

Baby you better break fast;
Let go of the past,
a fresh fate for it's never too late.

Wrong all along,
you can't do more prolong.

Thoughts tempted
to reflect, project,
but you feel it must reject.

Alive in lies,
the story is in your eyes;
I hope you realize.

Existing to Fight

We wonder why love
can't be the way it should;
No simple definition
only words of faith versus fear.

The closer we get,
the more it causes break;
Will our exit be a mistake?

Every news headline
has its end,
history repeated
and still trust remains defeated.
A puzzled existence,
is it worth the fight?
Will we ever unite?

Who are you to decide
what comes and goes?

Do you cease to cut our ties?
Or do we keep
from reversing our lies?

Hard enough to see
the way the world is;
Try to hope
but we shoot and miss.

Choose to smile away the pains,
it's you, it's me,
we go on displacing these blames.

Change facts
to meet a single's needs,
still, you watch
as your neighbor bleeds.

This On?

Do you want
what everyone can't get?
Idol nation,
believing money's tender touch
is the reversal to all regret.

To past time
or at the stroke of a finger,
you're able to hit the make believe switch.
What a relief to block out these signals
with one cola taste.

The bitter difference is equal to
an existing deceit,
gone with distorted sweet music
you play stuck on repeat.

There goes the boom in the drum,
like the projection of thunder
becomes a heart you did rupture.

The herd is unheard
as the crowd begins to grow waiting,
wishing you to speak.
Is this what you need,
a notorious profession?
Or never going to get lesson?

Away we go into space,
admiring the stars.
There goes the piano as it strikes,
like an eruption of lightning,
that discharge of a world dreaming.

Check one.
Check you.
This microphone on?

Eyes Write a Child's War

If I could write
the story of your life,
it would begin and end
by taking one look
in the color of your eye.

Like blue skies and ocean the same,
pages read blank
because characters could not change.
As mountains collapse
and the scene unfolds,
here will forever be
a part that your heart stole.

I come here
with the white flag.
Times tell war is obsolete,
'cause your every move
brings me down to a knee.

What I'm trying to say is,
I've fallen deeper than a star,
and one day my compass will connect
a warless heart to where you are.

The Life in a Kill

Why would you pick sides in war,
when it's you
that always loses more?

Like interest in a plastic holder,
selfishly needing today
and always regretting to pay later.

Empathy will gradually see
life through the black;
The person next to you
can clothe what you lack.

You can shoot and miss,
keep shooting when their body is laid
paralyzed on the ground;
Or you can put the firearms away,
hug to find a better way.

It's easy to feel
the life in a kill,
because if we continue to attack,
while forgetting to remove
those words stabbed in the back,
then we already lay here dead.

How about step
in front of your enemy
and give them a pillow
to rest their head?

If hate dominates
the world's circles
and forces a lost soul,
then combat will have us
at a reserved position
six feet deep.

Who will miss you
when you not wake from your sleep?

Now it's always do or die,
a spar between you and I;
When you comes before I,
you can inhale
while I exhale,
and finally, we can unwind suffocation
to see a sigh in excel.

This common air
is worth the movement
to mend awkward eyes
that cause a lie in our stare.

We lose and abuse
and when its time,
there is love to be had.
Who will be there,
move on to find you
with an open heart,
and implant faith
to never rip apart?

This is possible
made possible,
no one left liable.

You can't own
what someone else already has;
You can share this marble
that no human on their own
can simply handle.

Least not forget,
that when we unify
walking hitting the ground,
only war

can make a dead sound.

Is love a guilty silence?

The fight can't be
the same ole' voice
continuing to bury,
like the black mass singing
those countless prayers of a Hail Mary.

Breathe with Me

The air I breathe
is the same song we sing;
So whenever in doubt of another,
remember this ring:
Sure pain will come
and against it we stand,
today's cure resides
in grabbing a fallen's hand.

Days may die
at an early tide,
but look to the next
for too much it can provide.

Now, transfer spirits
and those memories to be held,
remember 'tis easy to revert,
but the past is what failed.

Imagine undiscovered trails
that can lead infinity,
maybe to a cross-road
exclaiming Trinity.

Verse

Let me sing a verse
that actually expresses
a true human's emotions;
Not one from celebrities' possessions,
that turns into little insecure boys'
and girls' Prozac obsession.

Let me write a verse
that lets them capture their dreams
without trying to be sexually obscene.

Music like poetry is an emotion
not a record label
corporate controlled notion.
It can shape and heal a heart,
absent of a chaotic vein potion.

Let me sing a verse
that doesn't steal souls
and drowns a kid for dollar
from sweat and tears.
While a host changes clothes
every hour on your favorite award show,
a family can't feed their breed
on a minimum wage.

Whether crack or some pharmaceutical pill,
death comes in more black and brown than in white.

Can't report death from wars overseas,
while every rap artist strays away
from unfoldin' American poverty.

In unspoken truth,
I guess that's a moral wrap,
and a government rap.
I dare music
to release the prison cells!

Suicide Car

From our war to it finding
its human deficiency, and
everything else blinded in between;
It's going nowhere fast.
How long will it take?
How many mistakes?

Change of channel
but it's all the same;
The faith and media attacks,
something wrong in the causality facts.

Cold campaign was never over,
stage of the evil roles
as towers being blown.
Sexualities unknown,
will the real acting ever be shown?

Liquid bombs,
endless tombs,
first black president,
and youth poverty proves
we ride unaware
in the same ole precedence.

Suicide car is going
no where fast,
as the peace white flag
can never be cast.

If not for mad money,
if not for greed,
we could stop our species bleed.

It has become an animal planet
on every single media outlet,
arguing to play the raped victim.

Pearl Harbor to 9/11,
60 years apart,
somehow it feels
like the same distance
from lungs to a removed heart.

Who will catch
a terrorist breath,
when there is no oxygen left?

Half way around the world
and back, seems to near;
Self-made IEDs
and a school shot up out of fear.
Domestic and the foreign
like every country
that used to rely on sovereign.
Too dependent,
too capitalistic,
it's modern day slavery
hidden like a magician.

I use to wake up,
oh decades ago,
problems unknown,
only worried about
the next cartoon show.

As time passed,
I see another countryman's suicide car
at an endless pass,
bringing life by frames
in a missing headshot.

Like a Presidential Lincoln
rollin' through Dallas,
I could be the patsy
or the Kennedy,
sittin' back
with a bullet to my brain;

Or the other standing at the library,
stacking study books,
while it's a race to get a shot off.

Like a heart beating rapidly
when the gun hand
is to scared to find peace,
who's going to run to the knoll with me,
absent of the slow start
to a Ruby nightclub conspiracy?

Watch

Anger is the last memory
before losing the one you love
at a blink of an eye;
Look up and then down,
split second the car wheel is gone.
Like the phone-remote,
we try to switch a scene
but nothings on.

Unlike the TV in you,
time can't fake it.
It will pass you up
like speeds of a flash bulb.

A snapshot controls a moment;
Determines a death to one's life,
and no words want to explain
what a last image told.
Will it be a lone breath history
and your tongue-less tragedy?

Today, I write for how
I feel the world's way,
and how yesterday
can be tomorrow's best friend.
In this presence,
we need to understand
love has no end;
For the way it is,
may never be how it was,
because we forget how this begun.

You take a look at your wrist,
when the one to watch
is next to you in the mirror;
You posses the change
in the hands of time.

Screaming Peace

Amaru in my front
and back pocket
for a go to move;
Here paragraph screens ring
like seas in typhoon change;
There is hide
and high tide terror age waves,
which tie to my heart-thug strings.

Will you take my shaking hand;
So we can grab a glass and
make a toast
for a language of disease?
For what is missing
in those that want to have
the whole world screaming peace;
Nervous body shots
shouldn't swirl in envy.

I know hate gets older
and younger at all the same times;
Love comes sometimes
in a so gone brother.
If this is a harder
than hard life,
then we're thankful to wake up
in the stone-cold morning.

God comes in every first blink
at those knocking on a frozen door;
On those hopeless nights,
when we cry for another
with puddle ice tears
on the wood floor.

We live in a last place home
suppressed like disc pinches
extremity nerves numb.

Here are poetic thoughts
chasing capital cowards
and their revelry bitches.

No Surprise Attack (United Speech of Infamy)

Surprise it's me,
no mask needed.
More than Plan B
'cause I actually map
a rebuttal attack;
for Trade Center equals
no Iraq, no Afghanistan.

I'm making up for
what every "peace" president lacks
since a Kennedy;
Remembering the troops,
remember what freedom took,
more than a 21 gun salute.

They stand here with me
at the podium
with an allergic war reaction,
waiting to explode
similar to the Manhattan project;
They're sneezing over the counter
like an antagonist of the Federal Reserve.

Now listen carefully,
I'm giving you a history lesson,
so don't question
what you think might be treason.
It's written,
as we keep dismissing,
missing Jefferson and Madison.

Look at our banks today,
currency interest strangling
our country under ransom,
singing got money like Lil Wayne.

Crooks should get fixed,
eliminate those of Richard Nix,

we can't forget the spirit of 1776!

Who is the real smooth criminal?
That's right leave the black
or white Michael alone.

It's politicians throwin' D's
into pockets for anyone
who provides oil,
into your car
and into your harden arteries.
Makes monetary sense
to want a job with these companies;
more than tax exempt in a corporate CEO.
Still overtaxing citizens,
we need another Shay's
this much I know.

So you question my creditability,
and the fight in me?
Well take one look
on the wall of over 'Nam's fifty thousand;
You can see Adame,
depositing the price of freedom;
The *tío* I will never see,
while you drone a child
who will never get to be.

Through the brick,
from the womb to the tomb,
if we don't protest now,
you will too see yours soon.

So you say
you got money to blow,
bottles to pop,
while soldiers are getting shot?
If that's America,
some founding fathers
roll over in their casket.

Ask not
what your country can do for you,
ask what?

You think you can rap?
You aren't 2Pac,
he was more like a poet,
and you should always be MLK prepared
to give your own life for it.

Think your ballin' but still
you're bouncing into a trap.

Laws telling me I can't have
a friend in Mary Jane,
when every prescription drug
drives a kid insane.
Providing pesticides
and vaccinating every thing
that comes from the ground;
Isn't that a shame?

Overweight, over drugged children
inflating their jean pockets,
and altering DNA,
while CEOs increase the fat in their pay.

You tell me to dream and fly,
but I get TSA x-rayed searched
all the way thru;
Michael Jordan never had that
when he flew.

You tell me to drop it low,
well I saw that at WTC and Hiroshima.

We forget to ask FDR
how you can lose 353 planes of a fleet;
Hard, right?
Like the fight in fat compounds of obesity.

In the lab
with a pen and a pad,
I got to study,
like it's 1929,
we have to find
a Ron Paul way out of
this depressin' insanity.

You don't need graduation
from me, you, or the educated;
only commitment
to a new course of action.

It has to start in the west,
not Kanye's steal the mic crap
but a different good morning.

Look at wars' cycle,
like on to the next one
in sounds of Jay-Z.
Whether war here
and over overseas,
rest in peace Malcolm,
and those who put their freedom of speech
on the X line;
For every life terror took,
let's light up a star every night,
as this anthem be the new
united speech of infamy.

Upon Us

I'm feeling kinda heavy,
can you please get off my back!
My spine and my mind
needs to grow,
like a skyscraper,
let me have my elevator in a temper,
the up and down of bipolar.

They say I have no street cred.
Well did you witness this,
what could have been?
A bullet through my family's vest,
from Nixon's and LBJ's Vietnam
to a father's copter crash;
Yeah, I'm crazy
from a military coup d'état influence,
PTSD from these blowback events,
and so far innocent.

I don't need to be
a marine to tell you,
how new world government took
a lone gunman shot at truth.

What I'm trying to do is
give you a voice,
when some have had no choice.

They've been sent to Iraq
to attack and back,
while you let magazines
redirect attention
to a favorite celebrity.

Coward politicians
use war to gather peace;
Oh please,
violence breads violence,

ask Michael Vick.

This RFK mindless menace
is a new terror war
I hear since 2001;
Well no weapon should bring fear,
and declaring independence
especially not be one.
Or it should not be some united stance
on a fighting something we can't see,
a tactic within, and something never-endin.'
Rights they take from
for a Bin Laden caveman
over by the Mediterranean Sea;
while building happiness off
emotional instability.
Today, we have to un-scatter
the meaning of this American dream.

Where is the 1960s
when people weren't afraid to fight?

Living day to day,
college loans and dead bodies
in our debt.
Smart TVs in endless supply
to keep the public away from having a notion.
Yes, you have us at our seat,
now I see the rise in obesity.
Let's watch a host dance
in forms of what is done to manipulate,
as there are no jobs left for a graduate.

What a shame,
experience doesn't matter.
You say a diploma,
some piece of paper
should start a career?

Mine begun in 1986,

and since, I've reverted to this:
Addicted to history,
like America to oil,
when you drop bombs
from the smallest airfoil;

I'll pull the trigger
in the strike of the pen;
How do you like a lead poising?

Oh he doesn't know war,
you say?
Or how to battle?
Well as long as
I got a tongue,
you can't take anything;
I'll speak,
until you collect all of BPs leak.

Don't get me started
on a having a post-college occupation,
until you end this imperial occupation.
Didn't you hear
of Rome and the British?
They tried it too;
for Jefferson is our prime witness;
Fighting wars from continents away
is dumb and so far from genius.
Look at the recycling history upon us.

Turn of the Ball (Your World, Your Court)

So you think this game is over,
because you're down
and you want to surrender,
but there is a fourth quarter,
like in a dollar.

Are we talkin' about
the turn of the ball or the money?
We're talkin' about true life,
a promise to never give in,
this is your world,
your court crowned by faith
that happens progressively.

Nothing can take place
unless you tell your soul again,
"This will never happen to me."

It's not that the one you love
doesn't care
or you lost them out of fear;
It's that we lived
brainwaves disorientated,
sometimes real,
and other times really overrated.
Lost by our inspiration
because we gave in
to that temptation;
turned living into a game
with no rules,
mannerism misconstrue,
but that really isn't you!

You have to fight on
by the seconds, because
life is redone in a flash;
The flicker will come as quick as
the blow in a whistle.

Waking up is a sign
to start that quarter over
or finish it stronger,
when you're cut up,
left for dead,
feelin' that feelin'
when you go to bed;
Know gentle sunrises
revolve for a reason,
another fight,
don't let your memories
own your life,
because you think over the things
you did late that one night.

Demons will dribble
leaving life to be like a scribble,
but when you've fouled out,
faith comes out of the temple,
and love will scream free
from the regenerated ventricle.

How will you draw
at the line enduring life's puzzle
that has your tongue
caught by the muzzle?

Blame only ourselves,
ask for a hand,
like the Lord says seek
and you will find,
cure the struggle
you have in your mind.

When someone steals your heart,
how will you sleep?
What is the fight
that you will keep?
How will they remember you
when it's said and done?

Will your idea live on?

Forget the questions
live by the answers,
let the quitters be
and remember the losers;
At one point we did win,
something more than a game.
How else did they get their name?

Want and Want (Your Attitude, Your Disease)

You want to secure power
when you can't control yourself.

You want to be heard
but you're not willing to listen.

You want to be loved
because there's a fear of loneliness
that can only be completed
by a life's witness.

You want to be saved on Sundays
when your forgotten faithful heartbeat
does not match your feet
throughout the week.

You want to drink
but you can't fill the emptiness
before it's time to pass the glass.

You want to take
but you can't find a way
to lend a hand.

You eat your riches
and you can't donate
to feed the sick.

You want to breathe
but you won't let the smoke settle.

You seek an immediate cure in drugs
before you can provide a simple hug.

You dream to be wanted
and you question the reasons for living.

You think you lay here dead

because you lost
the voice of resurrect.

No wonder why anxiety
overwhelms your sleep
when we live
like a brought to life disease.

When Heaven Cries

He's chasing us around,
statue too low to the ground;
Death is alive
in those anxious eyes,
as it comes
this is when heaven cries.

The child says,
"I'll never hold my own,
someone save me
before I drown."

A daily disgrace
dominate each step,
does he have anything left?
Feel and heal shattered hearts,
your refuge
would be an ideal start.

Truths are in
the youth we seek
but what kind of a peace
do I mean?
This world can't go on;
Too often we speak of free.
Is there an angel falling
inside of me?
He's called too many times,
and she ran out of sense.

As years to come
remain unclear,
we're conquered in bloodshed,
and our children cannot
continue to be misled.

Sometimes parents are here,
and sometimes

they will never be there,
either way,
we can't connect
because you are unaware.

Selfish minds
need not
build with a familiar sorrow,
begging for never knowing
in the fate of tomorrow.

SUNSET GENTLEMAN

Left to Dry

I know if I would leave you,
I would be out of the ocean
left to dry,
because everything in my world
wouldn't be right.

Hurting you
is the last thing on my mind,
for searching and searching
I would do,
knowing all you have to give
would be hard to find.
It doesn't matter
what you do,
all I see is me with you.

You taught me
how to fly,
how to believe
in you and I.
You saved me
from my life,
which was headed
down hill,
and instantly you knew
exactly what to fill.
You brought joy
and happiness in my heart;
It was only right
for us to never be apart.

Together what we have
makes life so true,
because surviving life
can only be accomplished
by having you.

I could go on

about what you do or say;
It's how you make
my heart feel in that special way.
The way my heart smiles,
when you're not around,
I know each feeling
is kept profound.

Eyes to the Sky

Corinthians sings,
listen to the iris building imaginary;
5, 4, 3, 2, to only one,
1 second shocked me alive.
Put me into
the shuttle she drives,
an orbital time,
a trip to pretend,
and the means to
another type of life end.

There is an angel
that God sends,
somewhere beyond
a distance galaxy,
a sling shot past reality.
People scatter
in the ship's rear background;
Forget earth,
leave it
at a parade of a cloud.

I'm flying;
I'll take the chance!

Bet it on
the wave of hello,
the wave of a cello.
Eyes to the sky,
listen to the chime!
When the music plays on,
this time it's okay to
erase gravity;
Swept off my feet,
off my fears,
her eyes will
hold on to me.

Put to Death, My Mystery {Daniel 2:03}

Be my eternal present,
so I could always
reside in heaven;
Every new day
would be an after life,
happily put to death,
and having you
as the only thing left;
Immortal at last
'cause each breath
will forever be kept.

You look great
from far away,
how does it keep this way?

The heavens
must triumph over hell,
as only blinking ticks will tell;

By accident or design,
I see one in each of her eyes.
While I let you break every rule
and evade every last dagger,
a man can't take it any longer.

Whether, washed away breaths
or smiles that made my day,
I said, "Never again,"
but it won't go away;
Guilty as charged
in dreams I see
and in diseased reality;
This mystery is our only mortality.

Like the currents that escape at sea,
tears are witnesses living in me.

Journey through you,
with you,
one day the crying floods
will discover treasure.
With your touch
I will have the world
at wet fingertips,
catching you,
and losing control
will be offset by these lips.

Angel Flash

Arms I need
and hands to hold,
work in progress
we've been told.

Listen as he speaks
with cries,
the river I built now
has watered my garden;
I live free,
without a burden.

All those years I died fighting,
today, he's got everything living.
From the start foolishly,
I fell apart;
With lies I crumbled
like a rock, today,
mountains lie in front of me.
Effortlessly, I break free.

With war, I empowered enemies;
Letting hostility arrest my heart,
now, this peace
can never be broken apart.

The sun will rescue
my moon as seasons go;
Weather and remember this alone:
Let angels flash with direction,
and with love
we must set eyes on above;
Not on evil on earth,
as he will capture you
until we find rebirth.

Some Forgiven

Before demanding a renewal,
some forgiven lifeline had to start.
She said, listen
to shade of this alarm,
it's tearing my skin,
lost never to be found
deep into the quaking rip
of a lonely heart.

Again, for his last time
an emergency falls,
because he deserved to miss
the siren in her calls.

Mending for mercy,
baby I'm sorry.
Screaming,
wondering where
a perfect heart can lie;
My forever dislodged
leaving the water dry.

This is something
he didn't want to hear.
What about us?
She said, baby I can't trust.
He laid by his knees
in digress, living out the pain,
and she survives
with her new happiness.

All this time, fairytale
only came alive in our head,
and now look
there's an empty bed;
A body drowning
in the blankets of fantasy.
Better of mistaken,

better off to ask
for a new end,
for I know my love
won't be brought to life again.

Vacuum

I'm going to miss you.
You carried me away,
one tide at a time,
lying on top of this cloud
with that never-ending
drowning blanket of fantasy,
and with pillows protecting
my uncertainties of reject.

I have to seize
some type of control
to get out of the faces
I fight in these sheets
and find an un-discovered planet's sea
to rest these tears.

I'll put aside the times;
I'm glad they've taken place.
One thing is certain,
you can't vacuum,
oh that never forgetting
snapshot of your undying face.

Friends come and go,
memories last,
a link that forces me
to cherish the past.
It drives us here,
up and down
from lonely overcast roads,
one direction at a time
weaving in and out of love.

I can say
I was never deprived of
your type of soul;
The stories that would have
never been told.

I can let you leave,
happily,
for when I turn the page,
it's known I can always flip back here.

Call a Friend

I pray for these moments,
when you come for me;
Through the goodbyes,
through the lies,
through the unclear choice,
over again I await your voice.

With losing lips
among idle inspiration,
I know tears maintain
and hands become too broken
from catching the rain.

At a state in need of a shoulder,
you bring sanity closer.
Absent of fear, you said,
"The world is our dictation,
no more manipulation.
Security I bring,
and when the clock shall break,
I'll be your escape.
When hearts stop their beat,
I'll send you an angel to meet.
Call your forever friend,
as I will be a wave,
which will never end.
I match any current, any sound,
in a sunny day and a hurricane.
Whether faint and unimaginable,
days will calm
when you call my name.
Happiness comes home
in one queue, at the shore,
begging for entrance
not a moment too soon,
I live with you."

Bridge

No matter the distance
in how many people I pass,
my memory bridges your face.
You never knew
the feelings in
what your eyes said,
or the power of a heart
as your only trusted friend.

The thing is
unspoken words never
make one have to feel alone;
When my letters
washed away why,
and how those many more oceans
were going to be built
by an angel's cry.

I walk each heart's
quaking continent
in search for a presence
with the climb of every rock,
but scared to hit
the sky's imaginary line.
Stuck on
the bridge to nowhere,
somehow getting closer;
You drive me,
you're in me.
I'm here;
I stay here,
replaying those depths
in my mind.

A Strike Out Loud (The Last Thunder)

At the swing
of falling apart,
on the thinning string
of a lonely heart,
where there is the end,
found a ground where I start.

Skinning the face to the bone,
striking out to find the love
I thought I could never own.
Voices I wish I spoke
lost my core's touch;
Her clip at my last feather,
I took a shot crashing down in fear,
oh, I thank God
for my insecurity
landing me here.

The last thunder
wept down the rain,
torched my soul
to light a whole new world;
From the tip of the sand
to an approach of a revitalizing star,
I once hung beneath the moon
to find where you are.

Made Of

Two lanes merge
onto an I-beam,
the forbidden sky of a dream,
from the bottom ocean
of an industrial bloodstream;
Perfecting the past
from any migrate pair of eyes
we'll choose,
and this is what
comes to find a view:

I'll show
what I am made of,
never doubt
the love I will give;
Unlock door number one,
behind is where truth shall live.
Made of steel, but if you bring
the high temperature,
chemistry proves anything can melt,
that's for sure.
You know what you desire,
no matter the elements
I posses the fire.
Your external beauty will bring
any man to his knees,
and your intrinsic spirit is what
every human badly needs.

Ignite your soul,
release your mind,
capture the moment,
one day at a time.

In sun fall,
I feel your pain;
In a nightmare,
I live your stress;

I'm armed with light
to get us out of any dark mess.

This love bleeds,
again heals;
Ultimately, it will lead
to a lost place
everyone wants to be;
One step back
to regain momentum,
reconciling diversity
to end resistance;
Reminding this divined motivation
shall be kept persistent.

Fire Fighter

The way you looked at me today
thru the drink of a glass,
maps built the X on your lips;
Kidnap like a pirate,
the fire lit a stick of bones,
melting and burning
a strike right to me.

Those flames
you must fight from a man;
The ones that couldn't understand.
The fire fighter
can extinguish
any competing desire,
for the world
you have set on fire!

I never thought of the how's
and the no's,
and I can't control
what you and I already know;
It was an unlikely notion
in my head.
I can sleep in
to only dream;
I know where I want to be.

Hot Glue Gun

You have him,
fantasy hits reality's gun
with a crush.
In its glimpse,
it's a wish,
staring off into heaven's space,
'cause I can't handle
the magic in your face.

Can I have a touch,
a feel of just because?
A once upon that will never be us!

You're more than a name.
I'm beyond
that script on that badge.
We are more than
a flicker that lights the flash.

I talk,
she walks;
I'm not worth her time.
Baby you…
My eyes will hold
like the gift of glue.
Smoke filled days overcast
the thought you left in my head;
The yes,
the right now,
I not ask
for a future in any wed.

Love Finds

Don't resort to violence,
don't rain in with vengeance,
as a reminder of fairness
here is your lesson:

Unstrap the restraint,
let fate be,
let in a release of these words,
and let love go first.
A Hallelujah is a timeless revolution.
Believe it when it hurts,
love doesn't hide,
it finds,
a resurrection,
once you endure the time.
It will be the radiance
to guide you to shore,
when you can't stand
to live in the dark anymore.
In this universe of a self-destructing
poetic curse,
love's sunset can find
a will to change
the reflection of a skin.
A will that can't be sucked in
by the straw of an unwanted world,
where these lips use to strangle
the life out of us.

Love is a moment movement,
be constantly listening to the beat.

As Long As

No matter the speed of the day,
I always try to get you to stay.
I will carry you and my belief,
as long as it will
no longer cause you grief.

I seek forgiveness and nurture,
with you I feel
I can take one step further.
When the world is crumbling
and I am on my knees,
tell me you will stand beside me;
Hold me up or tie me down,
kiss me until your lips are numb.
Love until your bones
become weak,
and hug as if your arms are
cemented around me.

The more I am without,
the more I realize I should not give in,
or maybe I am mistaken?

My wounds will not heal,
so I am prepared to cut God a deal;
Take me into your arms
and I will sacrifice possessions,
as longs as he corrects my obsession.
The story can't end,
more memories to create,
leaving a higher power to decide
our own fate.

Coloring the Crush of Love (The Story)

I wonder for those seconds,
why God brought on my aesthetic ability to seduce,
and intentionally, why her sun skin caused him to deduce?
It's a reverie to have a better half
without a repetitive entry into the wrong and the right,
and something has to have a relationship that we want to forever last.
How could she begin to like one color,
something I could not understand?
It's mostly black and lightly white,
a night and day adventure that left a hanging head of a man,
it was everything lying in a photo,
what he refused to be, to see.
Her drag only forced him to misbehave
in a spirit trying to break away
from the formulating grey.
Her color is all that begun to persist,
believing in her mind frame that troubled him to exist.
What happen to classic?
He lost all that was romantic?
Like the daily proof in the spin of the moon and the sun,
it's the truth that caused her rerun.
When the mind can't control the body,
it's her soul poetry couldn't forget,
focused only on her sexuality,
it can be a un-dying dare to disrupt his immortal honesty.

What Life Meant

What life meant
is more than one day
from sunrise to sunset.
Over and over,
dusk to the blink
in your waking yawn;
A promise to still love
when a heart goes down.
My living forever
displacing heaven's self doubt.
At a first ray of her shadow,
he could see a reason
for existence always pass in front.
Forgiven walks you let me take
inside the crack of your soul;
The kiss on your skin
that word's healing
could not control.

Lips cheek to cheek
and on top of the forehead
is a touch that did not need
anything to be said.
A mapped out direction
on your face,
a compass my suitcase
only felt home to;
What life meant is all of you.

Any description,
any resistance
always lied in eyes
the morning after,
under your makeup,
the Tasmanian fire to my feelings
rose like a natural disaster.
Oh my natural disaster!

The fold of your lip
to your nose
made more than the moon's cycle
at the strike of your smile;
No skyscraper can find
the bedtime stories you compile.

I never wanted perfect,
what life meant
is more than one day
from sunrise to sunset.

For every last sorry,
there is a thank you;
A moment of a new man's proof,
what life meant
is the woman in you.

Sunset Gentleman

I looked so alive
dressed in how
she wanted him to be me.
She said my exported soul
was like these unboxed Jimmy Choos,
leading her compass eyes
down to buried treasure
in what needed to be unlaced.

She knew her love laid
like a coin, two faced:
Me, an undying Sunset Gentleman,
versus him, an obverse burnout plan,
with these triangles
and vicious cycles!

My hands became
the cadent shore,
which held the sunset seas.
I'm here for the currents
and the tides,
thru calm and violent oceans
when a sun dried force begs his cry;

Don't lose hope
with an eternal wave
bounce in you and I.

Triangles and vicious cycles!
So blue, the water and her eyes,
there was no difference
in either nighttime skies.

Like a bird migrating
and crashing into a window,
displaced under a certain shadow,
her and him beginning
and ending not to call,

chasing a familiar season
of a tragic fall.

Is this her silhouette,
as black as her constant former
life's self regret?

Cut a feather,
cut the guano crap,
he dives from water to water,
thirsty and down to one final sigh.

Triangles and vicious cycles!
So blue, the water and her eyes,
there was no difference
in either nighttime skies.

While I am too
daring to drown,
conveniently sinkin' in
the opposite side of a frown;
Baby, I see your shape!
I see beauty in
a lonely two-way escape.
Can me and you
have our time of day,
like a colliding aurora horizon?

Can you undo
the tie around my neck?
Can you unbutton
my innocent breath
from your hand holding tight?
When you handcuff
my thoughts to the moon,
will you feel my dream
from my dark suffocating light?

Triangles and vicious cycles!
So blue, the water and her eyes,

there was no difference
in either nighttime skies.

Years shy of an adorn decade;
Look up, the sunlight
is at a final fade!
In new found world
fixes of cracks,
there shines sparks
from a kiss of the moon,
like your illuminating,
breaking heart,
the one I can bridge.
Thee is one honest chance
in a new morning star!

If you want more life,
more love,
tell the burnout plan
you had enough.

In a Heartbeat

In a heartbeat,
a vessel's S.O.S
disregards the distress signal,
when your palpitations
and their swirling waves
respond to a calming compass
in my mind.

In a heartbeat,
when your face
meets my eyes,
it thrust at the speed of light.

Blame the exchange
on the drum of the atrium;
In a heartbeat
becomes all we need.
You won't notice it
until it's gone,
when I can't feel it
or she can't hear hers.

In a heartbeat,
the blood is dripping,
sinking to the floor;
A rosary wine pours
until I can't see mine anymore.

Where did my feet go?

I may be Mr. Irrelevant,
but I know gravity
never fails me.

In a heartbeat,
it's a rhythm
we survive on;
The soundtrack of a life,

through shadowy imagery
and synthesizing sunlit nodes.

How can I ever
continue to illustrate
this one of a kind state?

In a heartbeat,
he tells me,
"Please cry, cry, cry,
it increases our rate.
Please laugh, laugh, laugh,
it does the same."

Human blood
architects impulses,
guiding us to where
we want to go;
That precious beat,
in the next last breath,
hearts will be endlessly dying
to meet you here.

i.l.a: Inspiring Love's Apsis

Weekend Made

Late at night, feeling through,
to avoid all the tears,
drinking and talking,
those two accessory wretches,
her Carpenter Eyes put light
to my photo cropped darkness.

Your body takes its shape
and moons bring our escape,
lovely woman,
you made the weekend!
Because normal days
laid too contiguous;
Everyone falling apart
meant falling into
the right moments' pieces.
In every dance song left witness,
for here is a person in every line,
a life in a word,
a keepsake for all those mistakes
that made good times shared.

It's our destination
along each letter,
for there is someone's smile
to remember,
where two locked eyes signed a place,
in your young and unforgettable face.

Couldn't Let Her Stay

She says she likes me.
Couldn't I resist another man's
claimed once upon a time girl?
Am I less human, do I belong
in this different rebound of a world?
She says she likes me.
Broken and paralyzed
like my father,
addicted to shouldn't have,
and bleeding for my better half.
If cheating finds a disaster
and happy ever after,
princes versus devils,
this is what a love story is?
Not my girl on this bed,
asking what's going on in your head?
When he catches blame
like a ground consumes
piled on dead leafs,
alone on our long away from home,
do you feel my hand on your heart?
If she says she loves me,
and screams reminisce in my mind,
this is and that was I love you!
What am I suppose to do
with the two?
Contemplate trust issues
and future self-hate,
or keep kissing my neck
until I feel numb,
and it's you asking one more night
to stay, can I come?

Every girl, a bad habit retreat,
like it's my last first time,
if she hit rewind,
it's a reminder someone's past
makes me feel this alive.

Four Songs (2 Hearts, 2 Worlds)

The difference between apathy
and telepathy
is a person's voice coming to me
in a lucid dream.
And somehow your mind is glued,
when she comes to life,
late night soul entwine,
I heard four songs.
I stopped
and look at her,
my dreams, the myth of
I had never lived at all before.
All the world seemed to die,
we were the last of the seas.
I cried two rivers, one flowed
in the memory of her dream,
the other laid still as it did drain,
soaked up from all her pain.

Show me how long reality runs,
the nearest channel
to the Hudson's city?
Evil mornings drowning
for hangover water,
no answer ring,
the drink to the end of the bottle;
But questions lied in lips,
down in her talkin' ventricle
starting a new cycle.

As high as the highest peak
of every city's tower,
a heart could relay a signal
from each of our beats' scream.
Four songs, and her lil' antidote,
orchestrated a sweet vessel's
home flickerin' inseam.

Are You Right Here?

Girl who you talkin' to?
Who's taking a picture of you?
Disappear, reappear,
Are you right here?
No Facebook,
is it the same new look?
Knockin' on a concrete jungle door,
can you come out and play?
Men love their Texas hold'em,
your southern take over game
of Where's That Smile?
Is your ex askin', and
somehow he forgets to address,
a man's world shouldn't morn
in an unnoticed denial.

How do you laugh?
Do you shred a new tear?
Are you right here?
How long will you be gone?

New age questions
inspiring love when we're alone,
keeping magnetic potion,
keeping me in site,
if he returns again,
girl don't pretend,
I'm right here,
don't you disappear, no no.

Florescence

Lyrically determine
to build the perfect picture,
for one look into
the sound of your name,
reminds me
of a revolutionary change.
I don't wanna brag about the woman
I'm upon,
Tonight it's only one;
I'm more than pride
but this is what I won.
I see you laying there with your eyes
slowly at a close,
talk and talk until we meet again,
don't move your head, stay, stay,
stay on that beautiful pose.
Most times a glimpse isn't enough,
soft envelope
to the ring in a cell phone call,
my florescence
when all my darkness seems to fall.

Say, say, say
this will be greater than a moment;
Say, say, say
surreal will won't be a steal.
Dear scars, scars, scars
find light this time,
a heart can heal, heal,
heal.

Invisible Love, My Sunset Sweetheart

Woke up from the inevitable,
someone telling me
the mail doesn't move,
how am I suppose to get these letters
for you?
Sporadic recording
from a speechless face,
the queen of creative lone gestures,
with folklore poetry schemes
and unreal, the king of jesters.
Every day,
I'm struggling for a word, it's like
a peace prize chemist having another
new drug for every rare cancer.
Surrounded by a cocktail rim of a cast
in this unforgettable heart,
the pound of a sinkin' feeling
to my stomach;
When her voice meets an ear
my blood lights up
like the city skies
But who can see it glowing?

Invisible Love,
disappearing after a good night hour,
does the ocean ever go quiet,
do sweets taste as good sour?
I'd recite day by day
to have your body say,
I want you, and I need you.
Is this how I get to you?
When you're gone
all these first colors I see
halt to simply black and white,
like Avatar's Pandora
reverting back to the times
of a 1960s fedora.
As she consults a new generation

of the finds and keeps,
surviving teacher
can I be where you lay
for your cry and sleeps?

Uncanny (Dreaming Until Our World is One)

If you never heard from me again,
is there a place you would go?
That room where it all began,
you were mine,
you were mine.
The touch of a warning heartbeat,
a shadow of our sun,
that day
we were holding hands as one.
Your whispers were to me,
the world will lie,
and survivors will sing,
jealous of the peace
you found with me.

I was lost in you on the first day,
and now,
this world is beggin' for yesterday.
Pleading to a knee,
throwing eyes to the city sky,
WHY, WHY,
WHY?
Who will wonder in the tired,
tired night?
Who will stay and fight?

Love Trapped (Home By Sin)

Trapped between the door
and something to say,
he waited
for the sound of a hand's skin.
One more rejection from a woman,
the same ole God plan.

I confess, I have been broken
from an inconvenient time,
trying to capture ghosts
line by line.
Poetry locks the beating
and denying,
how this
and that will never be enough.
Love was on the other hand
of a mom and dad fight;
packing bags
and hanging up phones,
they all made me feel
like we couldn't do this alone.

Wings winded home by sin;
God said blood would be poured,
and water won't cure the thirst;
I couldn't put myself first.

Gasoline in the house
and flames in the heart;
Given and taken, losing
and holding by the finger tips,
like piano strings for veins,
those colors slowly
washed out the music in my eyes.
Angels gave me this, writing
to get you home by sin,
and love trapped in water
where the river channels begin.

Without Touch

The dialogue was in the molecules,
lips to lashes
Vibrating inside my veins,
her electric eyes hit a switch within.
Every look set
another new lightning choreography
for the dance of my heart.

Without Touch Part II

I'm staring at the portrait of your face
in my mind,
wondering if you see the same mirror
in your eyes tonight.

It's only us talkin' about the stories
of when we met;
I'm spitting out words, trying to keep
your undivided attention.
Sunkissed skin in every woman
couldn't capture
your one of a kind soul.
I don't remember
what else there's to be said,
all I can feel is an electric touch.
I could play this one way,
it's easier to look away
and not give a fuck,
but I'm flooding my one true heart
to be your everlasting friend.
In life surrounded by world's hate,
it's your voice as a means
to a patient day's mad end.
I'm asking God
and I'm asking time:
Do you have to sleep to be wanted?
Is together alone
the closest thing to happiness?
Will my head
give in to my past's forgiveness?

There are times when I see you
and you're not there;
a woman has never been able
to hold me without touch
the way you do.
Your invisible chair
symbolizing happy frustration,

crackin' and rockin' the distance
in a little boy's dream coming true.

I

I want you to hate me
because I never knew a love;
I want to create a fire
to bring back those sweats
of when I wasn't enough.
I shot ugly text messages
as protective bullets,
something I not am.
I live with the haunting stories
of a cheating father;
God can you save me
from never knowing?
How bad is it to get up there?
Can you find me an angel
through the sabotaging smoke?
I think I heard her
when she first spoke.
There are times
when I script my own war,
lying alone in a struggle
of pushing away armory so mean.
But it's really not me.

Anger from a child
with insecurity from the bricks
and trash bags of my home.
This is not me;
this is what I trade with, like
a poker dealer at a Las Vegas hotel,
he'll win and he loses,
sending home gambling stories to tell.
My mom would say girls come
and go, God stays current,
and a real patient woman will stay
if she understands your torment.
Fears are as good as dreams, I hear,
lives are as good as recognizing
the lesson from the dead, I show,

for when I want to know
new versed prophecies,
her angel will rise above
his own self-implode smoke.

I Want to Know

Staring at the minute hand
while I pretend to understand
why time passes.
All of a sudden,
I blink and you appear
like a firefly on a sweet July night.
Austin to Astoria,
she's right next to me; I'm whispering
peaceful songs about *ila*.

If your heart
had one picture frame in its room,
would it be us captured
in the lock of a set of lips?
I want to know.

At a standstill
bare foot alone in the sheets,
does your mind allow your body
to drift towards me
like a sail in search for wind?
I want to know.

If I took a dip in your skin,
would I feel the warmth of the moon
and the sun?
I want to know.

Do you pour wine
when you shred your tears?
Or do your fermented smiles shine
in the dark
with all the pain you ever felt?
I want to know.

Do you imagine two beating hearts
in the collision of love to be made?
Minute after minute,

questions slowly become
like wishful artifacts for a new world.
Cheek to cheek
after I whisper in your ear,
please kiss me
until no space in our bodies answer
the questions to my fear.

As Long As It Takes (Taking Flight)

I don't need a song to tell.
I don't need a clock's ring.
I don't need a story to unfold.
What I need is your hand to hold.
If I could no longer hear,
if the hour glass ran
its last cycle out, and if
the pieces of every scene disappeared,
I would still remember
the feeling of a first kiss.

As long as it has taken
to find one moment;
as much distance
that has filled my heart,
I find stars
which surface on my veins,
when your touch brings the skies
down upon my skin.

Weekend Made Part II

Time has a new name,
proximity a different face,
your presence,
the finishing touch of complete.
My world a step closer,
your view a bit wider,
our shared wish,
inching towards a tangible vision.

I use to think the world
about this girl, now,
her world is tongue-tied, my world.
In this apsis, too many planets
and not enough lockets;
it seems
like far from yesterday to all those
thoughts which came before,
and today capturing her every space
is all I come here to adore.

In and out the labor,
picture painted like building bricks,
her jump rope around my heart;
keep it going, please no tricks.
Some boys say
the head to toe look is overrated,
but look at what I done and found,
in search towards a mercy coast,
she set every diary precedence,
the better than any man's most.
Any machinist could never keep up
with these keys,
and those many more linguists
ran out of ink.
Babe, you brought
new life to what I use to think.
I feel every beat,
a reminiscence of your beauty

to every century's poetry.
Is this possible?
The more I contain,
the more I take a deep breath
from this hand's blood rushing
to your skin's vein.
Kiss me here,
keep my kiss waiting
when I'm not there.
Do me a favor, and keep it going,
this is what bliss is,
my heart
on my perfect victim sleeve,
what I can't help,
yearning
for a same city live discovery.

Morning Eyes

Baby brown eyes look at me,
put your hands here
right on top of my burnout skin.
Two thousand 5, 6, 7, 8, 9
and now one next to the three,
where does time go?
I say up four atriums,
then into my lips
and finding yours;
what a coincidence.
Baby, baby I will put two hearts first.
Come closer
and look
at the made weekend's sky tilt;
Dark one moment in sheets,
and instantly lit from empire life
to this starving city.

Baby brown morning eyes is it me?
Blink one time,
blink to bring the world peace
equivalent to lucky dreams;
And time
as my deepest recognized envy.
Staring at your face,
waiting for the light,
3 am, 3 more hours
and here comes tomorrow's sun.
Here I am finding you
instead of usual pillows on the floor,
secretly asleep
scared for you to hit the door.

What's the Matter?

She tells me mind over matter,
or is it the other way around
to find her in this lonely town?
I'm going crazy,
like Civil War 18th century terror and
new world ambitions.
Woman tall, woman at the bus seat,
I'd search for her at every embassy.

Baby, where
did your childhood have you play?
Baby when you grew,
where did you go
on your father's sleepless nights?

Have I hit the smoke?

It's getting harder and harder
to reminisce of our burning fire.
I want to lose us
and find me among you,
somewhere in a museum picture
when they knew peace did exist.
I don't want to fight you,
nor blame disguises
on what God gave me
in my far from poetic past.
"He's too much,
this is too much," she says,
and after all the heat
the rain will wash in,
like tears spilling
on a man's foolish days.

Where are we now,
over your favorite hill,
then down the slate of failure?

She needed relief,
and I got my sensitivity
going our own two ways,
Baby, oh Baby,
let's not go back to these days.

In This Waiting Room (ila-Heart)

Oh...*i l a*...
Something great
for as long as a moment in life;
She was perfect like a Beatles' song
I couldn't let myself remember.

If my inspiration comes
from ripped out sheets,
and what she won't let me believe,
let it be; Sing to me
how good it feels to be alone.

Time is something
in forgiving the high blood
that comes to an empty rush;
I remember nose to nose,
the only difference in you with me;
Today, nothing is left to me?
All the electric current
in her city's cable couldn't un-fill
the darkness in this room.
Why won't this seed ever bloom?

Oh...*i l a*...
Beautiful-wishful lips
and their echoes do me tender,
the cries of her touch
on my skin project,
like a reminder at each fresh moon.
This is all we were?
Movie montages in the sky,
ripped out pages;
Or unwritten lingers in the sky?
Nothing to do in heaven,
the bigger her scene time,
the more these short hands will hurt,
only such secret irreversible eyes
can make an unfair heart.

Her Precipitating Mind

Haunted by the ventilating prayers
my grandmother left;
The only true sleep I've ever received
by rosary in the hand
and an unconscious camera flash.
Fast forward to the newest of times,
in any sort of calming friend,
I've learned vulnerability
is a man's best ex.
Crazy
like a pill in a tear drop shot glass;
I dissolved so deep
I wish I could
stay drowned like gravity.
Maybe never exist
for I'm washed away
by every woman's walk,
poured in new lust *Renaissance* writings
eclipsed by lonely nights'
drunken 3 a.m. chalk.
Her academic appeal
with a body's coat
that leaves psychosis heal;
Oh how your thoughts are still
dripping in
my precipitating mind.
How they'll live endlessly
in my black crown irides,
when it's mom asking,
who brings these cries?

Generational heartbreak
like the rain leaves that stay
fall after fall, proof in the season
of a clipped dove
and wind being absent of love.
Cold sleet flooding down,
head to the ground,

staring at the shadow
of those long lost friends,
and what was never said.

"Come closer faithfully,
fear none. We're together alone."

Wide open hearts
will perfectly shatter
like a vacant window rim,
and arms will remember
the slippery hands
recapturing a bird bath home.
When they ask
for an unmasked forever,
a good-bye is his tears and her
heaven's smile way of see you later.

Whispering Droplets to Ashes in the Wondering Sky

They sing
the sun will come out tomorrow
to dry these three locked tears,
each for day excursions, and
in all those yesterdays
deciding to be colorless one.
These kidnapped clouds
child'ed the river falling,
decoded through my eyes,
alone by sinkin' sands
with her cactus rose,
the lasting vision,
on his own without a ore,
a storm mistaken him for something
that isn't buoyant any more.

Age finds its true creation
after she's gone from days.
When paper turns piezoelectricity
to her throne shaped ashes
in the wondering sky,
will he be dismissed
like whispering droplets beating
on a charming clear window side
right before the full on rain?
He's looked upon
the ill-jazz world speaking
her body glass frame as new feelings,
can never die over repetition.
Will every free man's hand replace
its beautiful harmony key axis
on these living *noches tristes*?

In Every Desperation

Dear my happiness
in every desperation,
I'm lying over the desk resolute,
crushed
at the thought of getting
a realistic expectation from you,
and continuously pretending to feel
every person that walks to me.

Am I interesting only
when love isn't fair?

Babe, did you
go for what you knew all at once?

I'm trembling warm wrapped
in thinking about my mistakes,
and what your wander-embrace
gave me in the first place.
These silly restless sins
sold the distance in my head.
Where are you now?
Did I become obsolete language?
Will passion start to count
and look to me numb?
Or everyone else
in a perfect-run change?

Dear my happiness
in every desperation,
this is no time
for the blind insecure
by a meaningless shadow.
Screaming rays
won't ever set the same, and when
the hypnotizing flock of birds call,
your name can't help but be as silent
as when the leaves cover a trail

blazing in and out the darkest fall.

All these mindful moments
come in angels
at the wake of both our eyes,
by the cycle of sophisticated days
that say one too many goodbyes,
when we begin anew by a town's
morning bright, bright mercy.

Dear my happiness
in every desperation,
face to face,
I search for you between the walls
for six inches
to let me forget,
to let me fly,
to let me believe
there's something here
amongst the *Atacama* fire and
its incurable rain.

International War Memoir

The war memoir goes out
and countries collapse;
Is it heard,
an international anthem of longing?

She wasn't from New York,
but she produced
her own Broadway blues,
named Trapped in
The Contempt of What I Mean to You.
Her eyes sketched the blockade
of skyscrapers, matched with nuclear
Texas thunderbolts in a design
of cardiac veins;
at every human's rooftop view,
blooming arms and mouths
pointed in the direction of clouds
as north as Maine's.
A thousand trips couldn't find
her type of beautiful fallen star blend
and the knowing
became a sword-blade game.

When too many spaces
can't undo the cuts,
she is the lyrics the whole world will
never gasp enough air to sing.

This, an ugly tragedy,
her laurel and his red wreath,
trailing deeper than affairs fitting
November '63 dresses of Mrs. Kennedy.

She outdrew the paint
in each poet's hand,
these Aeschylus wounds stitched
attempt for cures
by the worst man she ever had.

Who Will Tell Me (Close Your Eyes)

Close your eyes. Mine will open
in trust of what will appear.
You're around,
but movements seem so wrong
when the beautiful waves are torn.
I'm headed in separate ways
with no one to chase me down,
only this tonic
and pearl sin in my hand.
When the flame ahead and behind
and it's gleaming instant change
come alive at the highest birth,
I'm water clinching
in everything that's done.
And who will tell me:
I shouldn't have kissed you.

I was in the dark of all this treasure.
What's gold when I can find
one too many hearts with no eyes,
in touch beyond the lies?
Spin me, take me, leave me,
this is it,
and back to a needless ready.
Did I let you control the ear too soon
from your self-made remedy?

These thousand mile tundra sounds
in my sleep seem
like premature sirens from
my past misused message in a bottle
and easy word punching throttle;
Knocked out cold
from the heaven snowslide cloud,
disposed here,
swinging like a playground child,
with some kind of cancerous cigarette
trapped in my sweltering finger tips,

feeling from the absent
more and more
less oxygen to my lips!

I didn't even know ya, took every
lonely sign from the country side,
and I found your precious pebbles
at the seabed of every ocean;
Some kind of secret to add
to this ungodly potion.
I tried to run, to hide with
diamond flashes in the heavy soil.
Shameless fantasy
short of permanent carbon ecstasy
like torn up freedom
with lung tight handle bars.

Close your eyes. Mine will open
in trust of what will appear.

If Love

Is there fairness that you have,
wooing n' stinging me from how you
and only you wanted?
Is it putting to rest
what you thought of me
for a better living written draft?
There was more than a musicless slow
dance under a summer Dallas night,
to laying down lips,
to beautiful pain whistling from
pressurized walls in the day after.
My If Love,
what would you say, if I asked,
In and out
a hundred country's cabs and inns,
can our locking hands;
can sounds of sidewalk kisses
house endless space between lungs?

Or is fairness your silence
if I find you today
and say, I still want you?
Your fulfilling thoughts
threaded and bedded a heart
which gave me chance
of what I could never become,
but everybody gives up to relive.
When you say in everything
there's a reason,
well, is there one for me wanting
to stay sewn in a dream,
never wake up
because it's as close to reality to die
in my miss and taken sleep?

Fuiste in every if love day,
suddenly,
we've become too far from there,

for fairness
is now never questioned,
from a honorary guest
at center of attraction, to searching
for my friendly congratulations
in your rarely answered digital glass.
If fairness had a disguise,
it begins at the smallest arteries
running the tissue
in your muscular soul,
then bouncing straight to mine
where I lie
towards earth's infinite cold.
This is pride, this is me, this is you,
rotating in once upon a time was
our Helios' palm nervous heat.
Now, I'm rocketship combust
to space's gravity free apsis,
wishing for one day to come home
by the dreaming memories of
inspiring love
that found something to exist.

She Is

When you meet a charming woman
and she is all the distance
replaying in your head,
it is not easy
doing those impossible things again.
What is it worth
to tell her how you feel?
For actions could never take place,
postcards, poetry, and an envelope
tracing and stamping hearts
as an only hope.
You begin to wonder if life is real?
Walking alone
seeing couples hold hands,
and a terrorizing world in ruins,
where there is one true good,
is where she is.
You can't be there,
what good is good
when it is killing him
in every body racing conversation.

Every plane in the sky
tells lonely people who they are,
waiting to come home
with deep patience;
Stay, what will stay,
She is worth all the distance.

*He who learns must suffer. Even in our sleep,
pain which cannot forget falls drop by drop upon the heart
until, in our own despair, and against our will,
comes wisdom by the awful grace of God.*

- Aeschylus

www.ingramcontent.com/pod-product-compliance
Lightning Source LLC
LaVergne TN
LVHW051040080426
835508LV00019B/1630